boilerplate CW00542657

Population, Settlement and Conflict: Israel and the West Bank

David Newman

Department of Geography,
Ben Gurion University, Beer Sheva, Israel.

UNIVERSITY OF
LONDON

 CAMBRIDGE
UNIVERSITY PRESS

QUEEN MARY AND WESTFIELD COLLEGE.
University of London

Published by the Press Syndicate of the University of Cambridge
The Pitt Building, Trumpington Street, Cambridge CB2 1RP
40 West 20th Street, New York, NY 10011–4211, USA
10 Stamford Road, Oakleigh, Victoria 3166, Australia

First published 1991
Reprinted 1992

Printed in Great Britain at the University Press, Cambridge

British Library cataloguing in publication data
Newman, David
  Population, Settlement and Conflict: Israel and the West Bank – (Update).
  1. Jordan. West Bank. Jewish settlers. Relations with Palestinian Arabs
  I. Title II. Series
  956.95044

ISBN 0 521 40804 0

Library of Congress catalog card number:
  Applied for

Cover illustration:
Arab and Jewish holy sites in close proximity in the heart of the Old City of Jerusalem.

Update

Update is a unique project in educational publishing.

The series is aimed at A-level students and first year undergraduates in geography. The objective is to demonstrate the relevance of geography for the study of the real world. *Updates* combine accounts of concepts and ideas with a fresh range of examples and especially significant and up-to-date case studies.

Written by experts in the field, *Update* is produced from the Department of Geography at Queen Mary and Westfield College (QMW) in the University of London. The editorial board contains expertise from both geography and education.

We hope that you find the series as stimulating to use as we find it to produce. The editor would be delighted to receive any suggestions for further *Updates* or comments on how we could make the series even more useful and exciting.

Roger Lee,
Editor, *Update*

Preface

The Arab-Israeli conflict has been a major focus of world attention for over forty years. Central to this conflict is the issue of the West Bank – occupied by Israel since 1967 – and the future and respective rights of both Palestinians and Israelis.

Population, Settlement and Conflict concentrates on the main points of conflict between the two peoples, set within a broader politico-geographical framework. Particular attention is paid to the issues of demography and territory. The analysis is brought up-to-date with a discussion of the implications of the recent Palestinian uprising (Intifadeh). The final chapter compares the wide range of solutions which have been proposed for ending the conflict.

A word of caution to the student. As in all conflicts, the analyses of events and facts cannot be completely free of statements which may appear contentious or value-loaded to either Israeli or Palestinian. This *Update* attempts to present the arguments put forward by both sides in the conflict. The suggested readings also present a balance between Israeli and Palestinian scholars. Students should follow up these readings and come to their own conclusions.

The author

Dr David Newman, is a graduate of Queen Mary and Westfield College, University of London. He received his PhD from the University of Durham and is now is Senior Lecturer in Geography and Director of the Urban Studies Division at Ben Gurion University of the Negev in Israel, where he teaches political geography. His research interests focus on geographical aspects of the Arab-Israel conflict, as well as the politics of planning in rural development regions. He has published *The Impact of Gush Emunim* (1985) and (with L. Applebaum) *Between village and suburb: New settlement forms in Israel* (1989). Dr Newman is an associate editor of *Geography Research Forum*, an annual publication devoted to current research in human geography.

Acknowledgements

The author is grateful to the following sources for the adaptation of material for this publication: Ya'akov Shilo and the *Ma'ariv* newspaper; Meron Benvenisti and the West Bank Data Base Project; the Jaffee Center for Strategic Studies, University of Tel-Aviv.

Many of the maps were skilfully redrawn by Edward Oliver of Queen Mary and Westfield College.

Contents

Figures

Tables

1 Evolution of the Arab-Israel conflict

Origins of the conflict

THE ARAB-ISRAEL CONFLICT has occupied a prominent place in the world political agenda for over forty years. In essence, the conflict focuses on the mutual claims by two national entities for sovereignty over the same piece of territory – Palestine/Israel. The roots of the present political conflict date back to the late nineteenth-century and the respective national aspirations of both Jews and Arabs. Swept up in the euphoria of nineteenth-century European nationalism, Zionism came to express Jewish nationalist aspirations for an independent homeland in which Jews would be free from persecution. The early twentieth century was also a period of growing Arab nationalism throughout the Middle East, with a fervent desire to be rid of the Ottoman rulers who had reigned sovereign throughout the region since the sixteenth century.

While some Jews sought their place in the European socialist and emancipation movements of the time, the Zionist movement was founded as a means to bring about full Jewish independence and statehood in their own, separate, homeland.

The term 'Zionism' came to depict a unique form of nationalism – one which encompassed the symbol of the territory within the name of the movement. 'Zion' derives its source from Old Testament writings and was commonly used in Jewish prayers throughout the centuries to remind Jews of the Land of Israel 'homeland', from which they had been physically separated for nearly 2,000 years. This powerful use of territorial terminologies and associations had the effect that alternatives to Palestine were never accepted by the Zionist movement for their future homeland. When Theodore Herzl – the founder and first President of the Zionist Movement – proposed the establishment of Jewish colonies in Uganda, the Zionist movement overruled Herzl and insisted on 'Palestine only' as the 'natural' homeland of the Jewish people, one to which they would 'return' after a 2,000-year exile.

From 1880 onwards, East European refugees began to settle in Palestine – then under Ottoman rule – and to establish agricultural colonies (Fig 1.1). Palestine was inhabited by an indigenous Arab population, concentrated in the coastal plain towns of Jaffa, Lod and Ramla and throughout the

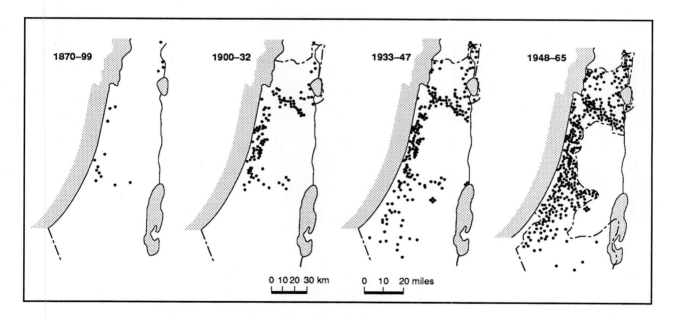

Figure 1.1   **Spread of Jewish settlement in Palestine, 1870–1965**
These maps show the gradual expansion of the territorial extent occupied by rural settlements established by Jewish immigrants throughout the twentieth century. While these villages, such as the *kibbutz* (collective community) and *moshav* (smallholders' cooperative), consisted of unique forms of social and community organisation, they were also influential in controlling ever-increasing amounts of territory for the Jewish state. Note how the pre-1948 pattern of Jewish settlement defined the eventual boundaries of the West Bank – a region virtually devoid of Jewish villages.
Source: Orni and Efrat (1980).

2

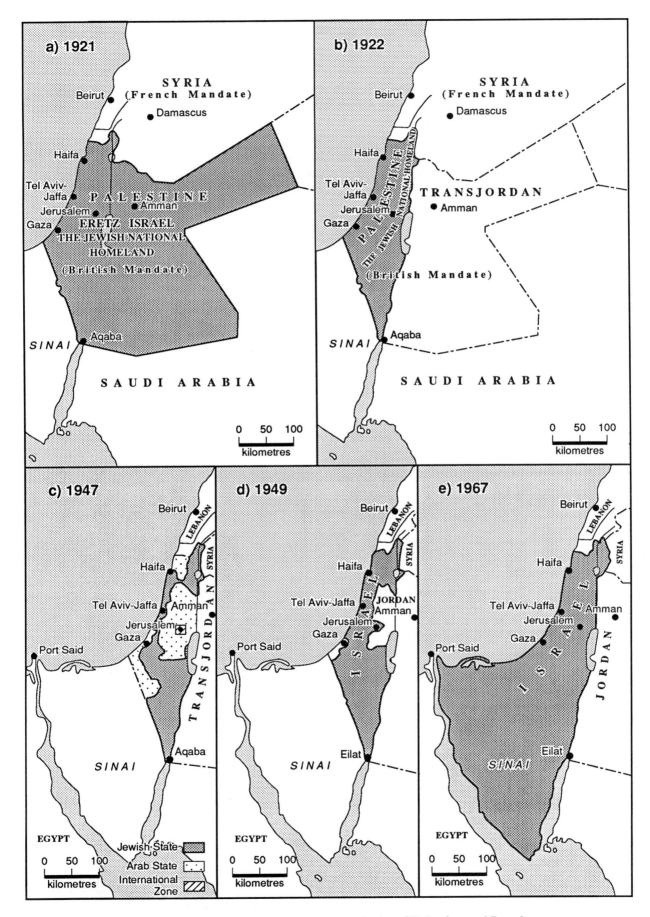

Fig 1.2   Sequential map analysis of the changing boundaries of Palestine and Israel

Figure 1.2a   Area of the British Mandate, 1921
The Mandate over Palestine was granted to Britain by the League of Nations in 1921. The northern boundary (along the present boundary between Israel and Lebanon) separated the British and French spheres of influence. The Balfour Declaration of 1918 (see text) referred to the granting of a Jewish homeland in this territory.

Figure 1.2b   The first partition of Palestine – the creation of Transjordan
The area under British Mandate administration known as Palestine was divided into two separate political entities in 1921, following the British decision to create the state of Transjordan on the territory to the east of the River Jordan.

Figure 1.2c   The United Nations partition proposal, 1947
On 29 November 1947, the General Assembly of the United Nations voted in favour of partitioning Palestine between a Jewish and Arab state. Under this proposal, Jerusalem would remain under international control.

Figure 1.2d   The boundaries of the state of Israel, 1949–67
The first Arab-Israel War erupted immediately following the establishment of the state of Israel on 15 May 1948. Following the termination of the battle in 1949, a series of separate armistice agreements were signed between Israel and her neighbours. The West Bank of the River Jordan was subsequently controlled by Jordan. The boundary between Israel and the West Bank became known as the 'green line'.

Figure 1.2e   Israel and the occupied territories, 1967
During the Six Day War of June 1967, Israel captured the Sinai Peninsula and Gaza Strip from Egypt, the West Bank from Jordan and the Golan Heights from Syria. The Israeli Knesset passed a law annexing East Jerusalem to Israel immediately following the War. A similar law was passed concerning the Golan Heights in 1982. The Sinai Peninsula was returned to Egyptian sovereignty under the terms of the Camp David Peace Accords between the two countries, enabling the demarcation of Israel's only internationally agreed boundary running from the Gaza Strip in the west to the port of Eilat in the extreme south-east of the country.

mountainous interior from the Galilee region in the north to Hebron in the south. While few of the early Zionists perceived their national movement as one that would dispossess another people, little thought or attention was paid to the existence of an indigenous population. It was initially believed, somewhat naively, that there was enough land for both peoples – especially as so much of it remained uncultivated and unused (at least by European standards) – and that the two groups could live peacefully side by side. Moreover, some early Zionists believed that the Arab nationalist struggle (against the last vestiges of the Ottoman Empire) made them brothers-in-arms with the Jewish nationalist cause. However, the gradual influx of immigrants and the increasing amount of land purchased and cultivated by them resulted in their being perceived by the local inhabitants as yet another outside European coloniser arriving to take control. This, at a time of growing Arab nationalist awareness and aspirations, was the root cause of the bitter conflict between the two peoples.

Jewish nationalist aspirations were boosted following the granting of the Palestine Mandate to Britain following World War I and the issuing of the Balfour Declaration in 1918, promising a national homeland in Palestine to the Jewish

people (Fig 1.2a). The final dissolution of the Ottoman Empire came about as a result of Turkey having taken sides with Germany during World War I. In the ensuing political vacuum, the allied powers decided to grant a 'mandate' to Britain and France to administer those territories previously under Ottoman rule, and to prepare the necessary political, social, economic and physical infrastructure which would enable the establishment of independent, self-ruling, states. France took over the administration of the territory which was later to become Syria and Lebanon, while Britain took charge of those areas which are today covered by Iraq, Jordan, Israel and the West Bank. The Zionist leaders believed that British rule would lead to the creation of a Jewish state, not least because the granting of the Mandate was followed shortly by the Balfour Declaration. This Declaration – in reality a short letter from the then British Foreign Minister Lord Balfour to Baron de Rothschild (a leading member of the European Jewish community) – simply stated that the British Government viewed the establishment of a national homeland for the Jews in Palestine favourably. This was interpreted by Jews as a statement of intent which would be implemented following the British takeover, especially as the British were committed to the establishment of separate states in the region.

Table 1.1: The Arab-Israel Wars, 1949-84

Year	Direct Combatants	Outcome	
		Territorial	*Demographic*
1948–49	Israel – Egypt, Jordan, Syria, Iraq	Creation of state of Israel and West Bank	Palestinian refugee outflow (*c*.700,000)
1956	Israel – Egypt	Israeli occupation of Sinai Peninsula and subsequent withdrawal	None
1967	Israel – Egypt, Jordan, Syria	Israeli occupation of Golan Heights, West Bank, Gaza Strip and Sinai Peninsula	Refugee migration from Golan Heights and West Bank
1973	Israel – Egypt, Syria	Disengagement agreements on Golan Heights and along Suez Canal	None
1982–84	Israel – PLO	Israeli advance to Beirut and continued control of southern Lebanon	Migration from southern Lebanon

However, the Balfour Declaration also made explicit mention of the fact that a national Jewish homeland in Palestine could not prejudice the rights of the Arabs already living there. The Arabs viewed Jewish immigration and settlement as a denial of Arab independence.

In 1921, Palestine was divided along the River Jordan. To the east of the river, the new Kingdom of Transjordan was created (Fig 1.2b) by the British and handed over to the Sherif of Mecca, who had been displaced from Arabia by the Ibn Saud family. The Sherif and his descendants were transformed into the Hashemite monarchy, which has continued to rule Jordan (at present under King Hussein) until the present time. To the west of the river, the whole of the region remained under British administration, and its residents became known as Palestinians – Jews and Arabs alike.

Tension between the Palestinian Arabs and Jews increased to the point of physical violence and bloodshed, the most notable incidents occurring in the riots of 1929 and 1936. British attempts to calm the fears of the local Arab residents culminated in the application of restrictions on further Jewish immigration and purchase of land for settlement. While additional newcomers arrived from Central Europe during the 1930s as a result of Nazi persecution, the rate of immigration slowed down following the British White Paper of 1939, limiting Jewish immigration to 75,000 over a period of five years and blocking further expansion of the Jewish territorial domain.

Israeli independence and post-1948 political events

Following the termination of World War II, the question of Palestine and the respective rights of Jews and Arabs was brought back into the focus of world attention. Committees appointed by the British government had previously proposed various forms of partition as a means by which both groups could be partially satisfied. In each case, these proposals were rejected by one of the two sides. Finally, in 1947, the British decided to leave Palestine and return their Mandate to the United Nations. In November 1947, the United Nations General Assembly voted in favour of partition between a Jewish and Arab entity, each of which would have full independence and sovereignty over their respective territories (Fig 1.2c). On the day that the British Government left

Palestine in May 1948, the independent state of Israel was formally established. The Arab states refused to recognise the legitimacy of this new state, a non-recognition which continues to this day in such diverse fields as international political, cultural and sports events; and the state of Israel is often omitted from maps of the area. Immediately following the declaration of Israeli independence, Arab armies invaded Palestine, resulting in the first major war between Israel and her Arab neighbours (Table 1.1).

Following the cessation of warfare between the new Jewish state and the surrounding Arab countries in 1948, the territory was ultimately divided between the state of Israel – encompassing the coastal plain in the west, the Galilee region in the north and the Negev desert in the south – and the 'West Bank', encompassing the mountains and slopes of Palestine, home to the majority of indigenous Palestinian Arabs (Fig 1.2d). This latter territory – separated from Israel by the 'green line' boundary – was administered as an adjunct of the state of Jordan for a period of nineteen years.

Between 1880 and 1945, the Jewish population of Palestine increased from approximately 25,000 to 600,000, eventually comprising some 33 per cent of the country's population (including what was to become the West Bank) on the eve of the establishment of the state of Israel in 1948. As a result of Arab refugee emigration and Jewish refugee immigration, the new state contained a large Jewish majority (see Chapter 3 on the politics of population). The country underwent rapid demographic expansion during the first decade of statehood, becoming the focus for mass immigration of the survivors of European Jewry following the holocaust, as well as the large Asian and African Jewish communities in Iraq, the Yemen, Egypt, Tunisia and Morocco.

The West Bank region contained a Palestinian Arab population numbering approximately 735,000. This figure includes nearly 300,000 of the approximately 800,000 (estimates range from 650,000 to 900,000) Palestinian refugees who fled from their previous homes during the fighting immediately following the establishment of the state – in itself ensuring the large Jewish majority within Israel itself. To this day opinion is bitterly divided concerning the question of responsibility for the mass exodus of Palestinians from Israel. While the Palestinians argue that they were

forcibly expelled by the Israeli forces, many Israelis argue that the majority of the refugees left of their own free will, urged on by their own leaders. Whichever version is correct (the truth is probably a combination of both processes), the establishment of the State of Israel not only created a sovereign national homeland for the Jewish people, but at the same time brought the Palestinian refugee problem into being. This problem remains at the heart of the ongoing conflict.

The first twenty years of the State were accompanied by much localised tension along Israel's borders with neighbouring states. Infiltration and terrorism were met by swift and severe retaliation by the Israeli military forces, resulting in a cycle of violence. In 1956, Israel – in collaboration with Britain and France – invaded the Sinai Peninsula, reaching the Suez Canal. Subsequent to American intervention, however, Israel was obliged to pull its troops back to the 1949 boundaries.

During the Six Day War of June 1967, Israeli troops conquered the whole of the West Bank (together with the Golan Heights, Sinai Peninsula and Gaza Strip), since when the region has been under Israeli occupation (Figs 1.2e and 1.3). The War arose out of a pre-emptive strike by Israel against her neighbours, in response to a perceived forthcoming attack by Egypt, Jordan and Syria. At the time, Egyptian leader Gamel Nasser had succeeded in joining the three countries' troops into an effective regional fighting force, and had closed the Straits of Tiran – Israel's only southern sea outlet to the Red Sea and the Indian Ocean – to all Israeli shipping. In addition, continual Syrian sniping from the Golan Heights into Israeli villages below, and occasional Jordanian sniping from the walls of the Old City of Jerusalem into the Jewish sector of the city, made Israel determined to take control of these regions. The Six Day War led to a further wave of Palestinian refugees leaving the West Bank, many of them second-time refugees who had found a temporary home in the West Bank during the previous nineteen years.

It is the West Bank region which is commonly perceived as constituting the territory of any future independent Palestinian state. For their part, Israel perceives the region as an important strategic asset and has undertaken activities aimed at ensuring long-term control over the region. These include

Figure 1.3   Israel and the occupied territories 1990: political and administrative divisions

While the specific problem of the West Bank cannot be divorced from the overall Arab-Israel conflict – both within pre-1967 Israel and between Israel and the other Arab states in the Middle East – the wider issues fall beyond the scope of this *Update*. Mention must, however, be made of the Camp David Peace Accords between Israel and Egypt (signed in 1979 and fully implemented in 1982) resulting in the return of the Sinai Peninsula to Egyptian sovereignty, thus once again changing the political map of the region (Fig 1.3). Events occurring in the West Bank will always have repercussions for the wider conflict, not least because the ultimate fate of the West Bank Palestinians lies at the very heart of any attempt to bring about peace in the region.

Summary

- The State of Israel was formally created in 1948, but the origins of the Arab-Israel conflict go back to the first Zionist immigrations to Palestine towards the end of the nineteenth century.

- Between 1918 and 1947, Palestine was administered by the British Mandate. In 1921, the British divided Palestine along the River Jordan, creating the state of Transjordan to the east. As a result of the Jewish-Arab conflict in Palestine, the British government 'returned' the Mandate to the United Nations in 1947. The UN voted for partition of Palestine between a Jewish and an Arab state.

- Since its creation, Israel has fought five major wars – in 1948, 1956, 1967, 1973 and 1982. In the 1967 Six Day War, Israel conquered the Golan Heights, West Bank, Gaza Strip and the Sinai Peninsula. With the exception of the Sinai Peninsula, all these territories have remained under Israeli occupation.

- In 1979, Israel and Egypt signed the Camp David Peace Accords. Under the terms of this agreement, the whole of the Sinai Peninsula was returned to Egyptian sovereignty by 1982.

the deployment of military forces and a continuing policy of settlement colonisation throughout the region. The local Palestinian population has grown to approximately 1 million inhabitants during the twenty years of Israeli rule, and has become increasingly militant in its resolve to force the Israelis out of the region and to establish an independent political unit. The conflict has come to the boil since late 1987 with the onset of the Intifadeh – or popular uprising – amongst the local Palestinian residents (see Chapter 7).

2   The struggle for territory

THE WEST BANK is an extremely small piece of land, covering no more than half a million hectares. The Gaza Strip comprises an additional 36,380 million hectares. Together, the West Bank and Gaza Strip (WBGS) is the home to over a million Palestinians (see next chapter) and approximately 120,000 Israeli settlers. However, the territory has a multiple role to play in the conflict and is perceived differently by the conflict participants. In this chapter, we will consider four alternative perceptions of the WBGS territory (especially the West Bank) in order to understand more fully the various policies adopted by the different groups. Territory will be considered in terms of its international status, as a strategic resource, as an economic resource and as a homeland.

International law and the occupied territories

Since Israel constitutes a sovereign state and is a full member of the United Nations, it is subject to the rules and guidelines laid down by various international organisations. With respect to international law, a distinction must be made between the pre-1967 territorial extent of the state of Israel and those territories conquered in the 1967 War. In the former case, the democratically elected government of Israel exercises full sovereignty over the entire territory and the peoples (Jews and Arabs) living therein. As explained in the previous chapter, sovereignty was attained initially through international recognition, namely the majority vote of the United Nations in 1947, and the acceptance of the extended boundaries (including the Galilee region in the north of Israel) resulting from the Arab-Israel War of 1948/49. As sovereign, the Israeli government has the right to develop the territory in any way it sees fit, subject to the rights of the individual and unfair discrimination.

Israel exercises no sovereign rights whatsoever over the post-1967 territories. Internationally, these regions are 'occupied territories', captured in war but not legally belonging to the present controller. A number of international conventions govern the activities of the occupying power in the occupied territories. Such conventions – most notably the Hague and Geneva Conventions – forbid the exploitation of natural resources, the expropriation of land for private or public purposes (*bona fide* defensive purposes are permitted on a short-term basis) and the transfer of population from one territory to the other. For its part, Israel differentiates between the occupied territories. The passing of laws in the Knesset (Israeli Parliament) formally annexing East Jerusalem (1967) and the Golan Heights (1982) to Israel has provided the internal justification for extending civilian (rather than military) law to these regions. In the case of the West Bank and Gaza Strip, no such laws have been passed and Israel does not claim sovereignty at present. These two regions continue to be governed (at least formally) by means of the military administration. Needless to say, internationally no distinction is made between the Golan Heights and East Jerusalem on the one hand, and the West Bank and Gaza Strip on the other – all are considered as occupied territory, to which the Hague and Geneva Conventions apply.

In this respect, it is worth noting that Jordanian administration of the West Bank between 1948 and 1967 was recognised only by two countries – Britain and Pakistan – as constituting the legitimate rights of a sovereign state. While the territory was not deemed as 'occupied' through an act of war similar to that applicable to Israel post-1967, sovereignty over the region remained undetermined until a future date. It is only in the most recent period (1987–88) that Jordan's King Hussein has finally given up the claim to some form of ultimate integration of the West Bank as part of the state of Jordan.

The only way in which Israel could ever be recognised as exercising legitimate sovereign rights over any of the occupied territories would be as a result of peace negotiations, in which such territories were ceded to Israel as part of an agreement. In a similar vein, the establishment of an independent Palestinian state in all, or any part, of these territories and its subsequent acceptance as an equal member of the United Nations would be a clear indication of Palestinian sovereignty. Thus the concepts of sovereignty and international recognition are closely interwoven.

8

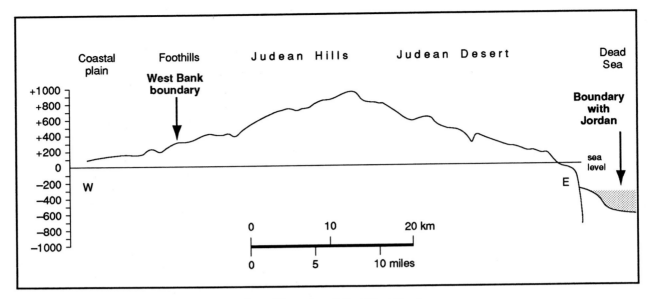

Figure 2.1   **Topographical cross-section of Israel and the West Bank**
The coastal plain lies within the sovereign territory of Israel (post-1948 boundaries) while the uplands are located in the West Bank. This territorial arrangement was perceived by many Israelis as constituting a major strategic threat to the country, in that army emplacements located in the hills overlooking the narrow coastal plain could fire on the Israeli cities.

Strategic considerations

Many Israelis view the West Bank as a strategic asset, providing a buffer zone between Israel proper and the neighbouring Arab state of Jordan. Living in a society within which the siege mentality and the feelings of constant threat are all-pervasive, Israelis argue that it is necessary to have some form of 'breathing space' between them and their immediate neighbours. Many Israelis point to the perceived danger of handing over the West Bank to Jordanian or Palestinian sovereignty as a move which would weaken Israel's physical security.

To understand the strategic argument we need, first to study the region's topography (Fig 2.1). Israel and the West Bank consist of a series of three longitudinal north-south belts running from Lebanon in the north, as far south as the northern Negev. The western strip consists of the coastal plain, varying in width but never wider than 15–20 km. It is in this belt that the majority of the Israeli Jewish population resides, especially in the Gush Dan metropolitan region around the Tel Aviv urban core. To the east of the coastal plain is the upland region, consisting of the Galilee mountains in the north, and the Samaria and Judea uplands in the south. The main residential concentration of the indigenous Arab population are to be found along this mountain ridge. To the east of the mountains lies part of the Syrian-African rift

valley, appearing in this region as the Beka'a in Lebanon and as the Jordan and Arava valleys to the south. A fourth north-south strip – again a series of uplands – lies to the east of the rift valley but, with the exception of the Golan Heights, this lies outside Israel, mostly within the territory of Jordan.

Before 1967, the distance between the 'green line' boundary separating the West Bank from the major Israeli metropolitan centres was less than 25 km, the shortest point being 13 km to the coastal town of Netanya (Fig 2.2). Moreover, the boundary itself runs along the lower slopes of the uplands, leaving the higher – and hence strategically dominant – points under Jordanian control, overlooking the Israeli towns and villages in the coastal plain. During the Six Day War, Israel captured the whole of the West Bank, thus pushing its eastern boundary away from the coastal plain, to the sparsely populated Jordan Valley. In a return to the pre-1967 borders, Israeli towns, it is argued, could be shelled with ease or, alternatively, a military offensive could cut Israel in two within a very short period of time.

A survey carried out in January 1986 by the Jaffee Center for Strategic Studies showed that 27.9 per cent of the 1,172 Jewish respondents believed that Israel should continue to hold on to the territories in order to prevent the establishment of a Palestinian state which would jeopardise Israel's

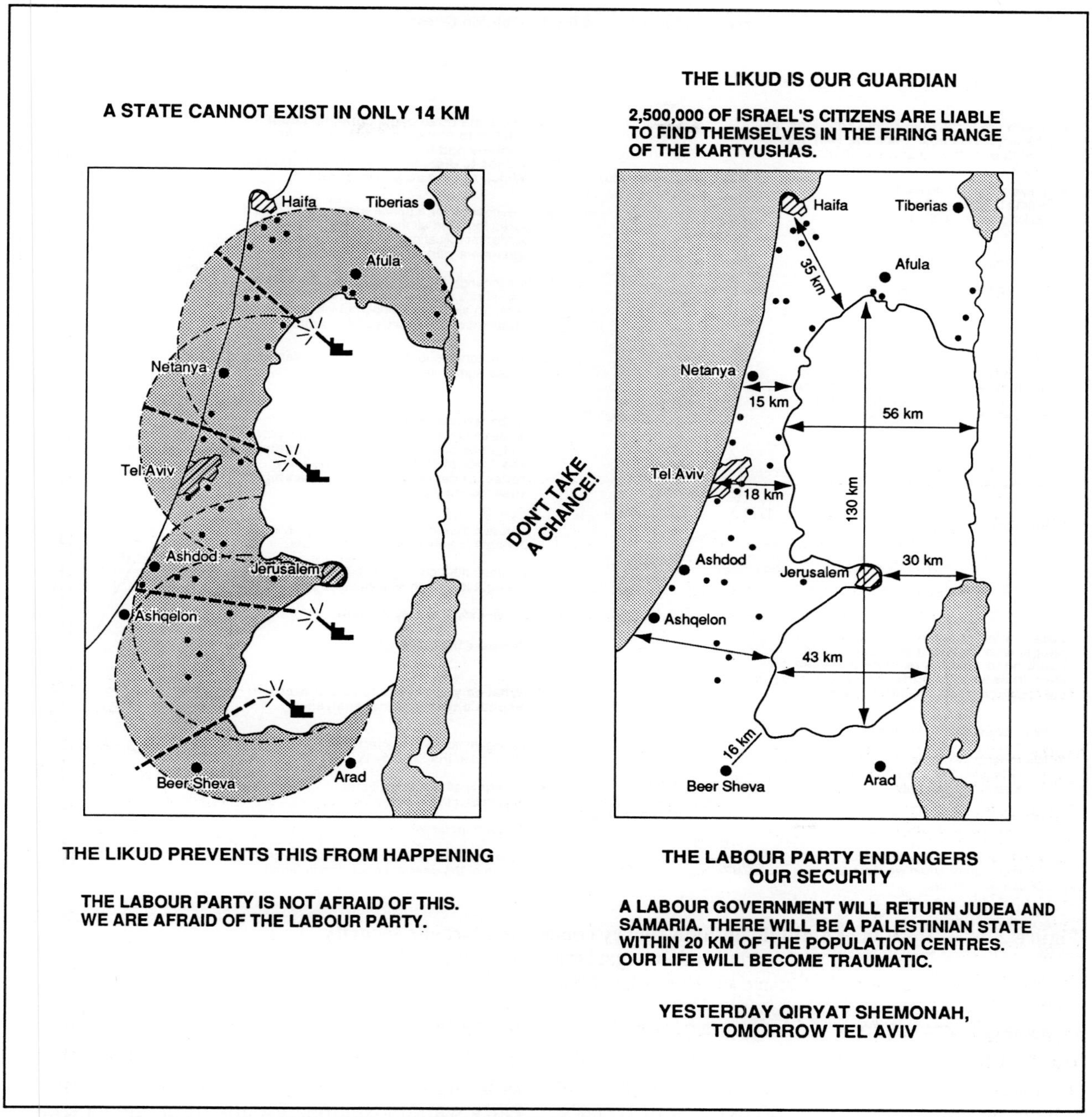
A STATE CANNOT EXIST IN ONLY 14 KM
Haifa
Tiberias
Afula
Netanya
Tel Aviv
Ashdod
Jerusalem
Ashqelon
Beer Sheva
Arad
THE LIKUD PREVENTS THIS FROM HAPPENING
THE LABOUR PARTY IS NOT AFRAID OF THIS.
WE ARE AFRAID OF THE LABOUR PARTY.
DON'T TAKE A CHANCE!
THE LIKUD IS OUR GUARDIAN
2,500,000 OF ISRAEL'S CITIZENS ARE LIABLE TO FIND THEMSELVES IN THE FIRING RANGE OF THE KARTYUSHAS.
Haifa
Tiberias
35 km
Afula
Netanya
15 km
56 km
Tel Aviv
18 km
130 km
Ashdod
Jerusalem
30 km
Ashqelon
43 km
16 km
Beer Sheva
Arad
THE LABOUR PARTY ENDANGERS OUR SECURITY
A LABOUR GOVERNMENT WILL RETURN JUDEA AND SAMARIA. THERE WILL BE A PALESTINIAN STATE WITHIN 20 KM OF THE POPULATION CENTRES. OUR LIFE WILL BECOME TRAUMATIC.
YESTERDAY QIRYAT SHEMONAH,
TOMORROW TEL AVIV

Figure 2.2 Perceived strategic threat from the West Bank
These two maps (translated from the Hebrew original) were used by the right-wing Likud party in the 1984 election campaign.

occupation of the West Bank was necessary in order to have strategic depth in the event of a war with Jordan (Arian *et al*, 1988) (Fig 2.3). In such an event, the West Bank would provide a buffer zone between Jordan and the Israeli population centres. Any battles would be fought away from the Jewish towns and villages. According to some sources, this argument had found backing in earlier reports drawn up by the US Military authorities in attempting to assess Israel's security needs (Fig 2.4).

Topography also figures strongly in this argument. As noted above, the 'green line' boundary divides the territory along the western slopes of the central mountain ridge, leaving the coastal plain and lowlands in Israel, while the uplands and hills overlooking the plain are located in the West Bank. This has become an important argument in the campaigns leading up to elections in Israel. Right-wing parties (defined, in the Israeli context, in terms of their hard-line stance on the question of territorial concessions rather than in terms of their position with respect to socio-economic divisions

National Security and Public Opinion Questionnaire
January 1986

9 There are three long-range solutions for the territories held since the 1967 war. Which one do you agree with most?

A In exchange for peace I would be willing to give up the territories as long as Israel's security interests were provided for

B Annexing the territories

C Leaving the situation as it is

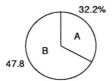

27 There are three basic opinions about the future of the territories in Judea, Samaria and the Gaza Strip if Israel comes to discussing peace with Jordan. Which opinon do you support?

A In exchange for a peace agreement, I would agree to return all the territories, with minor border modifications and with a special agreement worked out for Jerusalem

B In exchange for a peace agreement and for acceptable security arrangements, I would agree to return all the territories heavily populated with Arabs (about two-thirds of the territories)

C No territories should be returned, even for a peace agreement

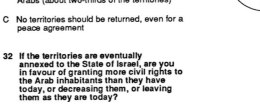

10 And, if Israel had to choose between the first two alternatives, which would you choose? (Only for those who answered C to question 9)

A In exchange for peace I would be willing to give up the territories as long as Israel's security interests were provided for

B Annexing the territories

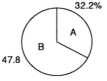

32 If the territories are eventually annexed to the State of Israel, are you in favour of granting more civil rights to the Arab inhabitants than they have today, or decreasing them, or leaving them as they are today?

A Increase their civil rights, including giving them the right to vote in Knesset elections

B Increase their civil rights, but do not give them the right to vote in Knesset elections

C Leave things as they are now

D Decrease their civil rights

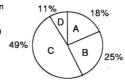

Here is a list of reasons used by some people who believe that Israel should continue to hold the territories. Please list them in order of importance. (Those who gave the answer as most important are counted)

A We have a right to the land

B We must prevent the establishment of a Palestinian state which could jeopardize our security

C We must have strategic depth in the event of war with Jordan

D We must have something to negotiate over when we discuss peace with Jordan

78 What do you believe to be the Arab aspirations in the final analysis?

A To regain some of the territories occupied in the Six-Day War

B To regain all of the territories occupied in the Six-Day War

C To conquer Israel

D To conquer Israel and annihilate a large portion of the Jewish population in Israel

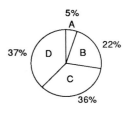

Figure 2.3 **Results of a public opinion survey concerning Israel's security**
The survey was carried out amongst Israel's Jewish population.
Source: Arian, Talmud and Hermann (1988).

in society) provide free, guided tours of the West Bank immediately prior to the elections. Sightseers are taken to points overlooking the coastal plain, in which are concentrated over 60 per cent of Israel's population. The impression is one of strategic domination and threat, necessitating continued Israeli control for the safety of the Israeli population. Left-wing parties – so the visitors are told – would return these strategic sites to foreign rule and thus endanger the Israeli civilian population in their homes.

The western margins of the West Bank are also viewed in strategic terms. The control of these hills by a foreign power would, so the argument goes, pose a strategic threat to Israel. The eastern approaches to the Jordan Valley must, therefore, be controlled by Israel as a means to ensure 'secure boundaries'. The present boundary between Israeli-controlled territory and Jordan

runs along the middle of the valley. Rising above the valley floor on both sides are striking mountain ranges, providing efficient look-out points and early warning stations for any troop movements on the opposite bank of the Jordan. The perceived strategic importance of the Jordan Valley as an easily defensible border lay behind the settlement concept enunciated by the Labour Party immediately following the Six Day War and known as the 'Allon Plan' (for a detailed discussion of this plan, see Chapter 4).

The strategic argument has been considerably weakened in recent years on a number of counts. In the first place, it has been argued that modern warfare has negated the need to control the border crossing points. The outbreak of renewed hostilities could be accompanied by long-distance missiles fired from Amman, Damascus or Jerusalem destroying the opposite cities. The

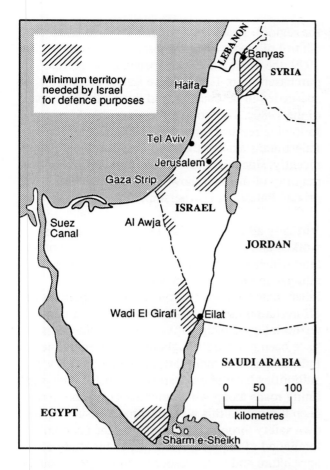

Figure 2.4   An American view of Israel's strategic requirements
In 1974, the US War College drew up a report concerning Israel's security requirements. In the course of preparing the report, a previous assessment drawn up by the American government in 1967 was uncovered.
Source: *Jerusalem Post*, April 1990.

lessons learnt from the Syrian penetration into the Golan Heights during the 1973 Yom Kippur War – and the evacuation of a number of Israeli settlements which were meant to be defending the border – has also brought into question the classic argument made by Israel that civilian outposts contribute to regional defence. The small extent of the West Bank territory also brings into question the perceived advantage of early warning time. For a fighter plane to cross the West Bank from Jordan (or vice versa) takes only a matter of seconds and cannot be stopped within such a small areal extent. This was highlighted as recently as October 1989, when a Syrian pilot, defecting with his MIG fighter plane to Israel, made an uninterrupted seven-minute flight into the heart of Israel. The one piece of territory which did constitute an important military buffer and early warning region was the Sinai Peninsula. However, this whole

territory was returned to Egypt as part of the Camp David Peace Accords of 1979.

It would appear that the strategic argument is important today mostly in terms of preventing the build-up of land forces or gun emplacements overlooking, or in close proximity to, Israel's coastal heartland. The Jordan Valley is a relatively easy border to patrol, while the control of the Samarian mountains enables observation of any troop movements. It would be logical to assume that under any future peace negotiations concerning territorial concessions, Israel would demand some form of demilitarised zone within the West Bank, together with a multinational or joint Israeli-Jordanian observation of the border crossing points.

In contrast to the West Bank, the Gaza Strip has no strategic significance whatsoever. This small strip of land is simply an extension of the undulating coastal plain, running from Israel in the north and continuing into northern Sinai to the south. Until 1967, the Gaza Strip had been under Egyptian rule, but was not included as part of the Camp David Peace Accords between Israel and Egypt. The population is composed of Palestinian Arabs who view their fate as being joined with that of the West Bank. Some Israelis argue that retention of the Gaza Strip is necessary in order to prevent the area becoming a base for armed infiltration into Israel, as had been the case prior to 1967. If, under a future agreement, a Palestinian territorial entity included both the West Bank and Gaza Strip, then the nature of the territorial link between the two regions – of necessity running through Israel itself – would have major strategic significance.

Land as a resource

For the indigenous Palestinian inhabitants of the region, the West Bank territory is essentially important as an economic resource. Approximately 30 per cent of the Palestinian residents (45 per cent in 1967) are engaged in agriculture or agriculturally-related employment. The terraced landscape of bountiful vines and olive trees is encountered throughout the region, except in the desert margins to the east and south. Of the West Bank's approximately 0.5 million hectares, some 200,000 are cultivable and another 200,000 consist of forest or grazing areas. Approximately 10,400 hectares of the total cultivated area is irrigated. While the area of rainfed arable land has been reduced during the 1980s, the area devoted to artificial irrigation has increased (Kahan, 1987). However, the latter has taken place mostly amongst the Israeli settlements of the Jordan Valley with the introduction of modern irrigation techniques in a region virtually devoid of precipitation. Palestinian agriculture in the West Bank does not make use of large-scale irrigation and is dependent on rainfall. The agricultural share of the West Bank economy dropped from 36.4 to 30.0 per cent by value of production over the period 1969–85, while the equivalent figures for the Gaza Strip were 28.3 and 17.8 per cent.

Israeli control of the region affects this economic resource in a number of ways. In the first place, the establishment of military posts and civilian settlements has often affected the ownership claims of local inhabitants. Both Israelis and Palestinians have their own version of the extent of land under private and public ownership, especially as regards Israel's right to ownership of state lands as the occupying power. For its part, Israel has assumed direct responsibility for all those lands – approximately 75,000 hectares – which were registered as state land under the Jordanian government prior to 1967. The total amount of land expropriated by Israel is disputed. According to a Palestinian source, Saleh (1990) argues that over 50 per cent of the total area had been taken over by Israel. In addition to the 'state' lands, this includes 50,000 hectares of unregistered lands, 32,000 hectares of land 'abandoned' by refugees plus an undefined extent of private lands.

There are also differences of opinion over what the occupying power is permitted to undertake on these lands. Both the Hague and Geneva International Conventions forbid the use of occupied land anywhere, for anything other than *bona fide* defensive purposes and even then the land has to be returned to the former owners once the defensive purpose is no longer relevant. Towards the end of the 1970s, a number of Arab landowners appealed to the Israeli high courts against the expropriation of their private land for the establishment of settlements. While the high court overruled their appeal – on the grounds that, within Israel, civilian settlement constitutes part of defensive policy – subsequent Israeli governments turned to the 'public domain' (lands considered to be the responsibility of the state) for most future settlement projects. In addition to 'state' land (constituting 25 per cent of the total land area of

the region), Israeli authorities have also assumed control of land owned by absentee Palestinians. In 1979, the West Bank was opened up to private purchasers from Israel. Some settler groups succeeded in purchasing land during the early part of the 1980s. This source has since dried up following reprisal threats on the part of local Palestinians against those willing to sell and, more recently, since the onset of the Intifadeh. The majority of the land, however, remains under private Palestinian ownership.

Virtually all the cultivable land in the region is worked and some of the terraced hillsides contain land which would be left fallow in other, richer, alluvial environments. In addition, the local inhabitants have learnt from the Israeli policies of afforestation used as a means of demonstrating territorial ownership. Olive trees and vineyards have been planted throughout the region by the Palestinians. For their part, the Israeli military authorities have often destroyed parts of orchards lining roads along which grenades or stones have been thrown. In this way, they have ensured their own safety through the removal of the economic livelihood of the local residents. In his study of agriculture and water resources in the West Bank and Gaza, Kahan (1987) argues that the uncertain political situation has led to apathy in local entrepreneurship and that most farmers are reluctant to invest in large-scale projects owing to the high risks involved. At the same time, there has been an increased transfer of land from field crops to vine and olive plantations. While there are good economic reasons for such change, the perceptions of orchards as providing long-term proof of land ownership is an additional explanatory factor.

A related, and as politically sensitive, a resource is water. Israel and the West Bank are located in a climatic region which borders the semi-arid. The eastern slopes of the central north-south mountain range lie in the rain shadow of the westerly winds. While the western slopes and the mountain ridge receive annual rainfall of around 500–600mm, the Jordan valley has an arid climate and must rely on irrigation for any agricultural cultivation. The West Bank is not connected to the Israeli national water supply system constructed in the early 1960s as a means of bringing water from the north of the country to the drier southern regions. Most of the West Bank settlements rely on local wells and underground aquifers for their water supply. Since 1968, there has been an increase of 33 per cent in

THE ISRAEL MINISTRY OF AGRICULTURE
presents:
ISRAEL – THE LAND AND ITS SIGNIFICANCE

THE QUESTION OF WATER – SOME DRY FACTS

Water is an extremely scarce resource in Israel. In fact, it is in many ways the limiting factor on the country's future development.

At present all the known sources of supply are being almost fully exploited – and in some cases even dangerously **overexploited.**

The country's natural water supply originates from three major sources:

★ The Jordan River catchment area

★ Two major underground water-bearing geological structures called **aquifers**

– The Mountain (or Yarkon-Taninim) Aquifer
– The Coastal Aquifer

The latter two sources constitute subterranean reservoirs, containing approximately 60 per cent of Israel's water supply. The waters they store are affected, directly and indirectly, by civilian and ecological activity in Judea and Samaria – as to both the quantity and the quality of the water.

The Physical Implications

★ Excessive pumping or uncontrolled sewage and waste disposal in Judea and Samaria are liable to cause serious *depletion, salination* and *pollution* of the aquifers. Relinquishing the western slopes of the Judean and Samarian hills will create a situation in which the fate of the national water supply could be determined by the actions of whatever Arab authority controlled the evacuated areas after withdrawal.

★ Any exploitation or pollution of the aquifers (particularly the Mountain Aquifer) by the **Palestinian** authorities would, by the principle of connecting vessels, have an immediate and significantly detrimental effect on the **Israeli** water supply. Given the present critical scarcity of water in Israel, even with **all** the

available sources of supply at her disposal, withdrawal and the relinquishing of control of a substantial portion of these sources could leave the country in a potentially desperate plight.

★ It is important to note that the mortal dangers implicit in such a situation could arise, even **without** there being any malicious intent on the part of the Arabs. They could result with equal severity from simple municipal mismanagement, poor planning, lack of knowledge or plain neglect. However, whatever the reasons may be, Israel might easily find herself facing irreparable damage to the supply of one of her most vital strategic sources – a situation which would, in a most tangible way, endanger her continued existence.

The Political Implications

★ The crucial issue to be considered in any political solution regarding the future of Judea and Samaria is the question of **who will have final authority in resolving issues in dispute.** This is especially acute in the case of water resources, as any proposed Palestinian political entity, whether sovereign or autonomous, would have no water resources at all, other than those upon which Israel is so critically dependent for her day-to-day survival.

★ This intense interdependence and the scarcity of water supplies accentuate even more the severity of the problem of **authority.** For under such conditions, even if some sincere and trustworthy Palestinian party could be found with whom an agreement could be made, the problem of allocating such a vital and scarce shared resource would make disputes almost inevitable.

★ Who would have the final say as to where drilling sites were to be located? How much water is to be pumped from them without irreparably damaging the aquifers? Where potentially polluting industries should or should not be established within the evacuated areas? In cases of disagreement, whose will is to be imposed on whom? How could Israel secure its vital interests without imposing impossible restrictions on the Palestinians' freedom to resolve their own domestic issues? Conversely, how could the Palestinians be given freedom to safeguard their legitimate domestic issues, without gravely endangering Israel's vital interests?

★ Moreover, even if all disputes were resolved, however unlikely such a possibility may be, and some fragile compromise were to

be reached, Israel's future would be completely dependent upon the honoring of that compromise agreement not only by the Palestinian party who **signed** it, but also by any **successor** who may come to power in the future. Clearly, the many extreme and militant elements, who undoubtedly oppose **any** agreement with Israel, together with the enormous socio-economic difficulties that any Palestinian administration would face, make very likely the overthrow of the original Palestinian regime and its replacement by some other regime, far more hostile to Israel. Such a successor regime would, of course, be highly unlikely to honor the compromise so vital to Israel's continued existence, especially as it would constitute the very justification for the overthrow of its predecessor!!!

★ Finally, relinquishing control over Judea and Samaria will leave Israel without any legal, moral or practical means to prevent the repatriation of almost a million Palestinians resident in refugee camps in surrounding Arab countries, whether by their own free will or by forcible "transfer" by their reluctant Arab "hosts." Such a wave of poverty-stricken humanity would generate an impossible strain on the already over-extended water supply and inadequate sewerage system, endangering even further Israel's vulnerable and fragile source of life.

★ It is difficult to conceive of any political solution consistent with Israel's survival that does not involve complete, continued Israeli control of the water and sewerage systems, and of the associated infrastructure, including the power supply and road network, essential to their operation, maintenance and accessibility.

This is an important point to ponder for those advocates of Israeli concessions who believe the Jews should have a viable independent state in their ancient homeland. It is important to realize that the claim to continued Israeli control over Judea and Samaria is not based on extremist fanaticism or religious mysticism but on a rational, healthy and reasonable survival instinct.

Presented as a public service by the Ministry of Agriculture

Figure 2.5   The question of water: a view from the Israeli Ministry of Agriculture
Source: *Jerusalem Post*, 10 August 1990.

14

the amount of water used for irrigation, with most of the existing local resources now being fully utilised. Total consumption by Palestinians is approximately 110 million cu.metres per annum, with a further 36 million cu.metres consumed by the Israeli settlements (Kahan, 1987). The use of these scarce water resources by Israeli settlements has further depleted the existing supply; approximately 6 per cent of the cultivated area of the Palestinians is under irrigation as compared with 69 per cent of the land in Jewish settlements. Some commentators argue that the scarce water resources of the West Bank are exploited by the Israeli authorities (see Fig 2.5) for use in Israel proper (Rowley, 1990b; Nijim, 1990).

Images of homeland

Both sides of the conflict perceive the West Bank territory as forming part of their national homeland. Amongst Israelis – and particularly the religious nationalists who make up the majority of the West Bank settlers – the West Bank constitutes the biblical heartland of the divinely promised Land of Israel (Fig 2.6). For them, the West Bank – or as they prefer to call it by its ancient Israelite name, Judea and Samaria – was 'liberated' and returned to its rightful owners in 1967 rather than being occupied by a foreign force. No non-divine decision – however democratic – can return this territory to foreign, i.e. non-Jewish, rule.

Similarly, many right-wing secular nationalists view the territory in historical – rather than religious/biblical – terms. They contend that this region formed the very centre of the ancient Israelite kingdoms that existed here until 2,000 years ago. For many of them, Greater Israel consists not only of the West Bank but of territory on both sides of the River Jordan (Fig 2.7). Both groups use a mixture of strategic and pragmatic arguments to further justify their case for retaining control over the region. They view the West Bank as belonging to Israel – by right – for eternity. In the survey by the Jaffee Center for Strategic Studies mentioned above, fully 48.6 per cent of the respondents argued that Israel should continue to hold the territories because 'we have a right to the land' (Fig 2.3).

For the Palestinians, the West Bank is the heartland of any future independent state. Assuming that no additional territory will be demanded from Israel within its pre-1967 borders

or from the state of Jordan, then the West Bank is the only remaining piece of Palestine on which an independent state could possibly be established. As in the case of the Israeli nationalists, the Palestinians view the territory as belonging to them by right – the right of undisturbed residence for centuries (Fig 2.8). Pragmatic considerations concerning the economic viability of a small, landlocked state, lacking many essential natural resources, is of only secondary importance to the basic demand for political independence on sovereign territory.

The mutual beliefs in homeland stretch beyond the West Bank boundaries and encompass the whole of Palestine. This is reflected in the use of semantics when referring to places according to either their Hebrew or Arabic names, each being mutually exclusive (Table 2.1). Israeli settlers

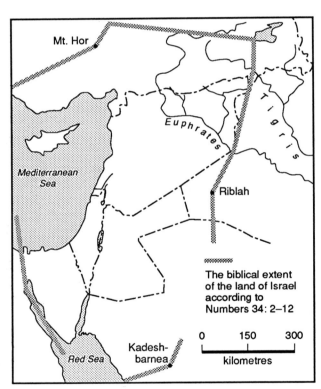

Figure 2.6 **The biblical extent of the Land of Israel**
Religious-nationalist groups in Israel claim the whole of the biblical Land of Israel as the God-given extent of the Jewish state. The territorial extent of this map (far larger than the present-day Israel and the occupied territories) derives its shape from the boundary descriptions which appear in The Bible - 'from the Tigris and Euphrates in the north to the large river in the south' (the 'large river' being alternatively interpreted as Wadi el Arish in the Sinai Desert or the River Nile).
Source: Isaac and Isaac (1976).

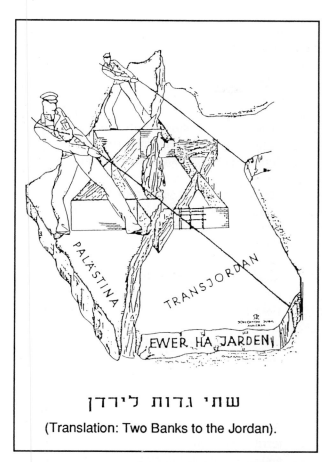

שתי גדות לירדן

(Translation: Two Banks to the Jordan).

Figure 2.7   The Herut image of Greater Israel
This map caricature was taken from a publication of the Herut youth movement (known as Betar) in the 1930s. It shows the right-wing image of a Greater Israel including both sides of the River Jordan. Betar members standing on the western portion of Palestine are using grappling hooks to try to bring back the eastern half (which, they claim, should not have been partitioned by Britain in 1922).

name the majority of the new villages after the ancient biblical names of local sites – a practice which serves to deepen the subconscious attachment between the settlers and the territory.

Despite their dispersion throughout the world for a period of almost 2,000 years, Jews retained a form of mystical attachment to the Palestine landscape. The cycle of the Jewish year, its holy days and festivals, as well as numerous sayings and quotations of the religious sages, were all based around the concept of the 'Land of Israel', a special, somewhat sanctified, territory, within which the Jewish personality could be fully developed. This conscious emphasis of territorial attachment as an integral element of peoplehood, has been described by geographer Yosseph Shilhav (1985) as constituting a form of 'territorial

indoctrination'. In their daily prayers, observant Jews constantly referred to 'Zion' (from which the term Zionism is derived) and 'Jerusalem', while a number of religious precepts concerned with agriculture and first fruits were discontinued since they were only applicable in the 'promised land'.

After such a long period of physical separation from the territory in question, the link between people and territory was psychological rather than actual. The physical return of Jews to the territory in question during the late nineteenth and early twentieth centuries, required the transformation of a metaphysical attachment into meaningful day-to-day behaviour. Thus, in an attempt to renew the link between people and territory – a link on which national statehood and sovereignty is based – they commenced the practical 'Hebraisation' of the landscape. In his book 'The Shepherds' War', Benvenisti (1989b) has called this process one of 'geographia sacra', through which many place names were changed in order to arrive at a Hebrew map of 'Eretz Yisrael' (Palestine). In addition, many of the religious precepts concerning agriculture and first fruits, which had been

Figure 2.8   The Palestinian image of Palestine
Just as the Herut image of a Greater Israel includes the whole of Mandate Palestine, so too does the Palestinian image of a past and future Palestine.

Table 2.1: The use of territorial semantics

Israeli usage	Palestinian usage	Place description
Jerusalem*	Al-Kuds	Town under Israeli control and capital city of Israel. Until 1967, divided between Israel and Jordan.
Hebron*	Al-Khalil	Town in southern section of West Bank – Muslim town which had a Jewish presence until 1929. Israeli recolonisation after 1967.
Judea-Samaria	West Bank*	Name for region west of the River Jordan, controlled by Jordan between 1948 and 1967, captured by Israel in 1967.
Israel*	Palestine	Region lying between River Jordan and Mediterranean Sea. Some Israelis distinguish between Israel in pre-1967 boundaries and the West Bank.
Administered territories	Occupied territories*	Alternative functional name for territories *occupied* by Israel in 1967 and subsequently *administered* by them.

* - denotes international usage.

discontinued in the Diaspora, have been reintroduced by observant Jews living in Israel.

Territory and national belonging: the essential link

This Jewish concept of territorial belonging is inculcated at an early age, taught through the medium of classes in *moledet* (alternatively translated as 'birthplace' or 'homeland'). Prior to the 1988 general elections, an extreme right-wing political party using the name 'Moledet' was founded, subsequently gaining two seats in the Knesset (Israeli Parliament). The conquest of the West Bank in 1967 reinforced this process of 'Hebraisation' and territorial attachment, not least because this mountainous region (Judea and Samaria) had been the very core of the ancient Jewish kingdoms, containing the holiest of places – the site of the Temple – in Jerusalem itself.

While many Israelis would argue that the 'Hebraisation' process was the result of a subconscious effort at changing the local landscape, Israeli Arabs and Palestinians argue alternatively that this has resulted in the deliberate obliteration of the local Arab landscapes and names. Arab geographer Ghazi Falah has termed this process, the 'Israelisation of Palestine human landscapes' (Falah, 1989), accusing Israeli geographers, and academics in general, of ignoring the existing Arab locale and society, as though Israel were indeed a nation state containing only one ethnic group. This debate is an interesting case of the inevitable introduction of political and value-loaded arguments into supposedly 'scientifically-objective' scholarly research. For the student, it is a good example of how most research within the social sciences cannot be value-free.

Indeed, the use of the terms 'Palestine' and 'Palestinians' to denote one side of the conflict is, itself, a post-1948 concept. Prior to the establishment of the state of Israel, the area was known as Palestine to all its residents - Palestinian Arabs and Palestinian Jews alike. For many years Israelis refused to recognise the existence of a Palestinian nation, composed entirely of

*Alternative forms of territorial control: **Plates 1 and 2** show the spontaneous growth of Bedouin settlement in the northern Negev region. Note the unplanned and ad hoc dispersal of prefabricated huts, each of which is located at a distance from the other. This enables extensive territorial control with relatively few inhabitants. The planting of orchards in proximity to the Bedouin encampments is a further method of strengthening the claim to the territory.*

***Plate 3** shows the Jewish response to the Bedouin settlement in the same region. The suburban settlement of Metar contains some 800 detached houses within a planned community. While this serves, to a certain extent, to form a wedge between the Bedouin encampments, the total area occupied by the community (each house is built on a plot of approximately 750 square metres) is equivalent to that occupied by no more than thirty Bedouin families. Note also the afforestation programmes which have been undertaken in recent years. In addition to the obvious 'greening' of the desert, the planting of forests is an important means by which public control of territory can be extended.*

***Plate 4** contrasts a small Israeli kibbutz outpost on the top of a mountain in the Galilee region, numbering fewer than 150 residents, against just one of the Arab 'villages' in the immediate region, containing over 10,000 residents.*

indigenous Arabs. As late as the early 1970s, Israeli Prime Minister Golda Meir is reported to have rejected any notion of a Palestinian people. Yet it is clear that a well-defined Palestinian nation exists today, having evolved at the same time, and partially in direct response to, the Zionist nationalist aspirations. The latter point requires some clarification. Juval Portugali (1988) has argued that nationalism in general, and Zionism in particular, is a generative process. By this he means that the existence of one powerful national idea generates a response from others most affected by its implementation. The emergence of a clearly defined Palestinian identity has come about, partially in direct response to the feelings of discrimination which have arisen out of the implementation of Zionism in the form of a

national state and Jewish sovereignty over the region.

Thus, in effect, the conflict arises out of the presence of two national groups residing in one territory, but formalised within the framework of a Jewish 'nation state'. This requires further explanation. Mono-ethnic nation states – that is, states within which there is only one national group – are few and far between. The concept arose out of the evolving nationalist feelings of ethnic groups throughout Europe during the nineteenth century. It reached its climax following World War I and the award of independent state territory to many small national groups. The concept 'nation state' is, in effect, the drawing together of nationalism as a social construct and territory as a spatial construct. The concentration of a single national group in a well-defined piece of territory gives rise to demands by the former for sovereignty over the latter – hence the state concept. It was against this background that Lithuania, Latvia and Estonia all achieved independence, the Kurds and the Armenians were promised independent state territory (which they never received), and the Balfour Declaration (see Chapter 1) was issued on behalf of an independent Jewish state.

But, as noted above, in the case of Palestine the nation involved did not reside in its national territory, despite the concepts of national territorial limits and ideas passed on through centuries of religious and historical teachings. Even following the mass immigration of Jews to Palestine during the twentieth century, there always remained a strong local Arab presence (which formed the majority until 1948). Thus, despite being defined as a 'Jewish state', Israel is in reality a bi-ethnic state. Israeli Arabs form a significant minority which increases substantially when the West Bank and Gaza Strip is included. The implementation of the extremist solutions offered by the banned Kach political party of Meir Kahane, as well as those of the Moledet party (see above), namely the expulsion or 'voluntary transfer' of all Arabs residing in Israel and the occupied territories to other countries in the Middle East, would bring about the formation of a nation state in which the Jews would constitute the only ethnic group residing in the national territory.

Summary

- The West Bank territory can be viewed from a number of perspectives. The strategic perspective is held by many Israelis, who argue that the return of the West Bank to foreign (Palestinian or Jordanian) rule would endanger the physical security of Israel.

- The Palestinian residents of the West Bank view their home territory more in terms of a resource, enabling agricultural cultivation and control of water sources. In addition, this territory forms the core of a future independent state.

- Both Israelis and Palestinians have different images of the West Bank territory as constituting their homeland to which they are attached. The Jewish attachment arises out of historical and religious factors, while the Palestinian attachment is based on centuries of uninterrupted residence. Each view the whole of Palestine as their rightful home territory.

- The Gaza Strip is neither a strategic asset, nor does it bring strong emotional attachments to the fore.

- The concept of a nation state is based on the concentration of one ethnic group in a specific piece of territory. Although Israel is defined as a nation state (for the Jews), in reality it is a multi-ethnic state, comprising a significant Arab minority.

3 The politics of population

As NOTED IN THE FINAL SECTION to Chapter 2, few states in the world are completely mono-ethnic. Most countries consist of a number of national or ethnic groups. Self-awareness of belonging to a specific ethnic group may be determined by a number of factors, the most important being: the size of the group (especially as a percentage of the total state population); the regional concentration of the national group (as opposed to dispersion throughout the country); and feelings of discrimination as practised against the group. The extent to which each group is fully and equally integrated into the state as a whole largely depends on the nature of government and the distribution of power throughout society. In a fully democratic society, we would assume that all groups are capable of being equally represented (although it does not necessarily mean that they exercise that power).

Nation and state: politics and population

In the case of Israel, the problem is twofold. On the one hand, Israel is defined as a nation (Jewish) state, even though it contains a significant non-Jewish minority (approximately 18 per cent of the population). The formal statistical term for this minority is 'Non-Jews' but in reality it includes Muslims, Christians and Druses. Of these, the Muslims constitute the vast majority of the non-Jewish population.

When the West Bank and Gaza Strip is included, the minority percentage rises from 18 to over 30 per cent. While Israeli Arabs share full voting rights and could, theoretically, elect as many as fifteen members to the Knesset (Israeli Parliament) under the Israeli system of proportional representation in a single nation-wide constituency, the West Bank and Gaza Palestinians are not citizens of the state and do not have any voting rights. One of the reasons, it is argued, that even the hard-line Israeli governments have not formally annexed the West Bank and Gaza Strip is precisely because they would then be faced with the problem of a greatly increased Arab presence within the Israeli Knesset, were the WBGS inhabitants to exercise their new voting status as full citizens.

Moreover, the problem is intensified by the differential natural growth and immigration rates of the Jewish and Arab populations. In addition to temporal variation, the demographic balances vary according to the geographical scale of analysis: Jewish-Arab ratios within the pre-1967 boundaries of the state of Israel (a large Jewish majority) are significantly different to that of Israel and the occupied territories. Similarly, sub-regions within pre-1967 Israel – such as the Central Galilee region – have a strong Arab dominance, as contrasted to regions (such as those around Tel Aviv) which are devoid of Arab residents.

From Table 3.1 we can see the changing population ratios for the period between 1948 and 1987. During this period, the Jewish population comprised a clear majority of the national population. This was due to two major migratory factors: the establishment of the state of Israel in 1948 was accompanied by a mass out-migration of

Table 3.1: Jewish and non-Jewish population ratios in Israel, 1948–87 ('000s)*

Year	Total	Jews	Non-Jews	Non-Jews as %
1948	914.7[+]	758.7	156.0[+]	17.05
1955	1,789.1	1,590.5	198.6	11.10
1960	2,150.5	1,911.3	239.2	11.12
1967	2,776.3	2,383.6	392.7	14.14
1975	3,493.2	2,959.4	533.8	15.28
1980	3,921.6	3,282.7	638.9	16.29
1987	4,406.5	3,612.9	793.6	18.01

* Excluding West Bank; East Jerusalem is included from 1967. [+] Figures for 1948 relate to the period following the mass Arab exodus of that year.
Source: Data are drawn from various tables in the *Israeli Government Statistical Year Book* for the year 1988. Published by the Central Bureau of Statistics (CBS), Jerusalem.

Palestinian refugees from their former homes within Mandate Palestine (for explanation of this concept, see Chapter 1). It is estimated that approximately 700–800,000 inhabitants fled the country for neighbouring states, especially the West Bank region and the state of Jordan. Subsequently, during the late 1940s and early 1950s, Israel experienced a mass in-migration of Jewish refugees from throughout the world, especially from countries in Asia and Africa, as well as displaced survivors of the European holocaust. Approximately 850,000 people arrived in Israel during the period 1948–56, more than doubling the Jewish population of the country.

The net result of these dynamic population movements was the consolidation of a strong Jewish majority within the state of Israel. In an effort to dilute the regional concentrations of the remaining Arab population, many of the new immigrants were sent to settle the country's peripheral regions. Newly established farming villages and development towns were founded throughout the Galilee and Negev regions as a means of population dispersal. By 1967, the overall Jewish-Arab population ratios within Israel had reached 85:15, varying between 98:2 in the Tel Aviv metropolitan region to 48:52 in the Northern District (including the Galilee region) and 35:65 in certain sub-districts (Table 3.2). In 1986, there were 770,000 'minority' (the official term) residents within the pre-1967 boundaries, equalling some 17 per cent of the country's population. These were dispersed throughout the three major Arab residential concentrations in the country: approximately two-thirds live in the Galilee region, a quarter in the 'Triangle' region in the centre of the country – hugging the old 'green line' boundary between Israel and the West Bank – and a further 60,000 Bedouin in the Negev region.

If we also take into account the fact that natural growth rates (the net difference between birth [fertility] and death [mortality] rates), are far higher amongst the Muslims than the Jewish population (Fig 3.1 and Table 3.3), then these ratios are likely to change even more in the

Table 3.2: Jewish and non-Jewish populations: regional differentiation, 1948–87

	1948 ('000s)	%	1972 ('000s)	%	1987 ('000s)	%
Israel (pre-1967)						
Total	872.7	100.00	3,147.7	100.00	4,406.5	100.00
Jews	716.7	82.12	2,686.7	85.35	3,612.9	81.99
Non-Jews	156.0	17.87	461.0	14.65	793.6	18.01
Northern District (including Galilee)						
Total	144.0	100.00	4,73.9	100.00	732.4	100.00
Jews	53.4	37.08	2,55.7	53.96	357.0	48.74
Non-Jews	90.6	62.92	2,17.6	45.92	375.4	51.26
Acco Sub-district (within Northern District)						
Total	54.7	100.00	193.4	100.00	312.0	100.00
Jews	6.0	10.97	72.5	37.49	109.2	35.00
Non-Jews	48.7	89.03	120.8	62.46	202.8	65.00
Israel+ West Bank						
Total			3,770.3	100.00	5,244.2	100.00
Jews			2,686.7	71.26	3,612.9	68.89
Non-Jews			1,083.6	28.74	1,631.3	31.10
Israel, West Bank + Gaza						
Total			4,149.1	100.00	5,789.2	100.00
Jews			2,686.7	64.75	3,612.9	62.41
Non-Jews			1,462.4	35.25	2,176.3	37.59

Source: See Table 3.1.

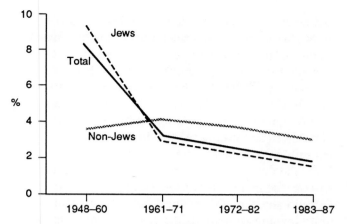

Figure 3.1 **Annual average population growth: Jews and non-Jews, 1948–87** (natural growth + migration)
Source: See Table 3.1.

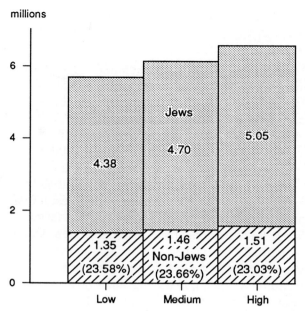

Figure 3.2 **Population projections for the year 2010**
Source: See Table 3.1.

immediate future. In terms of the classic demographic transition model, Israeli Jews (with the exception of orthodox groups who oppose any form of family planning) is entering a post-industrial phase of low birth and death rates, with only relatively small growth; Israeli Arabs and Palestinians are experiencing high birth and low death rates, characteristic of the industrial phase of rapid demographic growth. Figure 3.2 indicates projections made for the year 2010, all of which show the non-Jewish population component rising to just under a quarter of the total population within the pre-1967 boundaries.

Figure 3.2 requires some interpretation. Firstly, the demographic trends outlined above could change. On the one hand, owing to events elsewhere in the world, Israel could be the recipient of new waves of mass Jewish immigration. The recent removal of restrictions to emigration from the Soviet Union, coupled with restrictions placed by the United States government on the number of Soviet Jewish immigrants it is prepared to accept, has resulted in a significant movement towards Israel. During the period from June 1989 to December 1990, between 100,000 and 200,000 Soviet Jews found refuge in Israel. The multiplier effect of such a migration flow (which is now expected to reach a million during the 1990s) could

Table 3.3: Natural increase amongst Jewish and Muslim populations in Israel

	Births	Deaths (per 1000 population)	Natural increase	General fertility rates	Median age
1955–60					
Total	27.7	6.2	21.5	117.6	
Jews	25.6	5.9	19.7	105.3	no data
Moslems	46.3	8.0	38.3	250.1	
1975					
Total	27.7	7.1	20.6	112.5	
Jews	25.0	7.4	17.6	98.7	no data
Moslems	46.3	5.6	40.7	221.4	
1987					
Total	22.7	6.7	16.0	95.1	25.5
Jews	20.5	7.4	13.1	85.9	27.8
Moslems	34.3	3.4	31.0	149.0	17.0

Source: See Table 3.1.

significantly change the future demographic balance between Jews and Arabs.

An additional factor to be taken into account is the changing behaviour of Israeli Arabs and Palestinians. As each of these groups become more fully integrated socio-economically, if not politically, into the modern Israeli capitalist economy, it is reasonable to assume that their fertility patterns will experience a marked decrease. Indeed, in some sectors this is already beginning to show. Such change would result in a more favourable demographic balance as far as Israeli Jews are concerned. While this latter factor has partially been taken into account in the preparation of Fig 3.2, this is not the case regarding a sudden, mass migration flow. Thus, despite the indication of an ever closing gap between Jews and Arabs, there are many unknowns which may radically alter these forecasts.

The figures used to construct Fig 3.2 include the Palestinian inhabitants of East Jerusalem. East Jerusalem has been formally annexed by Israel,

and hence its inhabitants are viewed (by Israel) as belonging to the state. Thus all demographic data and projections for Israel as a whole tend to include the East Jerusalem Palestinians. It should be noted, however, that the residents of this part of the city do not view themselves as Israeli citizens (see Chapter 6). They continue to identify themselves as forming part of the West Bank Palestinian population under Israeli occupation. Were the demographic forecasts to be recalculated, without the inclusion of the East Jerusalem Palestinians, then the results would, once again, be more favourable towards the Jewish demographic majority in the long term.

Demography post-1967

The occupation of the West Bank and Gaza Strip in the Six Day War of 1967 resulted in a changed demographic balance. The Palestinian population of the West Bank (including East Jerusalem) immediately following the War numbered approximately 650,000, while a further 390,000 resided in the Gaza Strip. Subsequent to the fighting, a significant proportion of the West Bank residents fled, as refugees, to neighbouring Jordan, many of them as second-time refugees (thus explaining the negative growth figures for 1967 in Table 3.4). A further 100,000 Arab residents of the Golan Heights had also left the region following the Israeli conquest, leaving a small Druse population in the north of the Golan close to the Syrian border. Despite the refugee out-migration from these areas, the inclusion of the Palestinians who chose to remain in their homes meant that the new Jewish-Arab population ratio in a 'Greater Israel' underwent an overnight change from 85:15 to 70:30.

While no census of the Palestinian population has been taken since 1967, the Central Bureau of Statistics estimates that the Palestinian population of the West Bank (excluding East Jerusalem) has increased from 586,000 to 858,000 between 1967 and 1987, an increase of 270,000 – or 46 per cent in twenty years (Table 3.4). This has not been a uniform annual growth, ranging from 2.4 per cent per annum in the early 1970s, decreasing to less than 1 per cent around 1980–81, and rising to a high of 2.7 per cent in 1984. These figures take into account high natural growth rates and a net negative migration balance (more Palestinians leaving the region each year than arriving). In recent years there has, in fact, been a greater

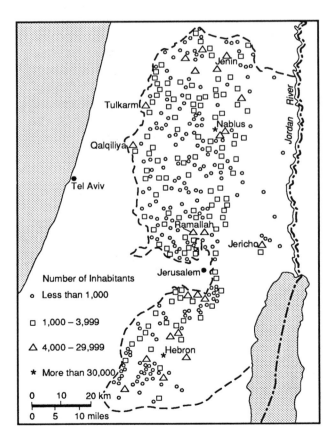

Figure 3.3 **Distribution of West Bank Palestinian inhabitants, 1967**
Source: Benvenisti and Khayat (1988).

Table 3.4: West Bank population growth, 1967–86

Year	Total population ('000s)	natural increase ('000s)	% annual growth
1967	585.9	13.0	-0.5
1975	665.2	18.6	0.5
1980	724.3	22.9	0.8
1986	837.7	27.5	2.7

Source: See Table 3.1.

Table 3.5: Population projections for the Palestinian population for the year 2002 ('000s)

	West Bank	Gaza Strip
High	1,428.7	992.3
Medium	1,210.8	865.5
Low	1,060.5	741.1

Source: Benvenisti and Khayat (1988).

tendency on the part of the Palestinians to remain in the West Bank than was the case in the 1960s and early 1970s. Their distribution is shown in Figure 3.3.

The figures in Table 3.4 do not take into account the growth of either the East Jerusalem or Gaza Strip Palestinian populations. The former have increased from approximately 137,500 persons in 1967 to 271,500 in 1987 – a growth of 97.5 per cent – while the figures for the Gaza Strip show an increase from 380,800 inhabitants in 1967 to 545,000 in 1986, an annual increase reaching 3.4 per cent in recent years. The reader should also be aware of the fact that the West Bank Data Base Project (an independent institute for monitoring change on the West Bank since 1967) argues that the above figures, based on Israeli official statistics, are underestimates. Their own figures – based on field surveys in West Bank villages – indicate that the Palestinian population (again excluding East Jerusalem) increased from 583,227 in 1967 to 1,067,873 in 1987 – showing a twenty year increase of 83.1 per cent.

In contrast to the case of East Jerusalem, Israel has assiduously avoided annexing any other part of the West Bank or Gaza Strip. This has been as true of the more moderate Labour governments (who

believe in ultimate territorial concessions as part of a peace agreement) as it has of the hard-line Likud governments (who desire to retain these regions under Israeli control). The possible demographic threat to the Jewish majority of the state of Israel as a consequence of such annexation has been perceived as too great a risk, especially with the extension of full civilian (and hence voting) rights to all inhabitants of the annexed regions.

Population projections for the West Bank and Gaza Palestinian populations indicate a significant increase by the year 2002 (Table 3.5). Moreover, the fact that nearly 70 per cent of the Palestinians in 1986 were under the age of 26 (the median age for Muslim citizens of Israel is only 17 – see above, Table 3.3) means that the overall demographic ratios between Jew and Arab within a Greater Israel will – at the present pace – continue to work towards numerical equality over a period of approximately fifty years, to be followed by an Arab majority. It is thus understandable why all Israeli governments, of whatever colour, have refrained from formally annexing the territory to Israel.

Instead of a policy of *de jure* annexation, the Israeli administrations have implemented policies which have resulted in *de facto* annexation of the West Bank. The territorial implications of Israeli colonisation policy are described in the next chapter. However, in demographic terms, approximately 70,000 Israeli settlers now reside in a variety of urban and rural settlements dispersed throughout the region, in addition to an equivalent number of residents in the new urban neighbourhoods of East Jerusalem. Allowing for an average of 4-5 persons per household, this gives us around 25–30,000 households who have settled beyond the 'green line' boundary in the twenty-year period since 1967. It should also be remembered that a high proportion of the West

Bank settlers are young, religious (orthodox) families. As such, they oppose any form of family planning or contraception and are likely to increase their average family size well beyond the national (Jewish) average.

The Jewish presence in the West Bank can be viewed from two alternative perspectives. On the one hand, the absolute number of settlers and their families represents a significant population movement which has taken place in a relatively short time period. Alternatively, the sum total of Jewish residents throughout the West Bank remains small when compared with the sum total of the local Palestinian population. In the West Bank (excluding Jerusalem), the Israeli settler population represents only 8 per cent of the total population, and this figure is much lower in the Gaza Strip. Moreover, while the reservoir of Israeli citizens prepared to relocate their homes over the 'green line' has been largely exhausted, the local Palestinian residents continue to experience high natural growth rates. In addition, fewer of the young Palestinian adults are now leaving the region for other countries. As a result, the relative gap between Israeli and Palestinian residents of the West Bank is likely to grow in the immediate future.

Summary

- The demographic balance between Jews and Arabs changes according to the geographical scale taken for analysis.

- Within pre-1967 Israel, Jews form the vast majority (approximately 82:18 per cent), although Israeli Arabs form the majority within specific regions, most notably the Galilee region in the north of the country.

- Over 1½ million Palestinians reside in the West Bank and Gaza Strip. Since these territories have not been formally annexed by Israel, the inhabitants are not considered as full and equal citizens. Were the territories to be formally annexed, then Israel's Jewish majority would be considerably decreased.

- Differential rates of natural growth between Jews and Arabs work in favour of the latter. As such, the gap between the two population groups (at whichever scale examined) will slowly decline.

- The current influx of mass Jewish immigration from the Soviet Union is expected to redress this balance in favour of the Jewish majority.

4 Israeli settlement policy

THE MEANS BY WHICH a government brings territory under control are varied. In countries where there is a consensual democracy, control is by agreement and all citizens participate equally in the political life of the country. In situations of conflict, where a minority is governed by a dominant partner, other means of control may be put into use. The most blatant form is a crude military control based on the use of force. Many governments have chosen to use variations on the theme of colonisation as a means by which to effect their control over minority regions through a civilian, rather than a military, presence. This form of control has a long history and can be seen as far back as the Roman Empire, in its attempts to integrate far-flung regions into the dominant culture of the Empire. That does not mean to say that such policies are always successful (success being measured in the eyes of the controller). More often than not, the intrusion of a new ethnic group into a region results in inter-group tension and violence which may continue for centuries. Protestants in Northern Ireland, Turks in Cyprus, the French in North Africa are just a few examples of the long-term implications of policies of settlement colonisation.

The use of civilian, especially agricultural, settlement plays a unique role in the Arab-Israel conflict. Settlement has been a key element in the expansion of Jewish control over Palestine (pre-1948); the consolidation of that control throughout Israel (1948–67); and, more recently, in attempts to establish long-term control over the West Bank and Gaza Strip (post-1967). Sociologist Baruch Kimmerling, has discussed the importance of creating a civilian 'presence' in the landscape as an important means of ensuring long-term control, especially in circumstances where the land cannot be purchased legally ('ownership') (Newman, 1989). Such was the rationale behind the so-called

'tower and stockade' settlements which were founded in the course of a single night by Jewish settlers in the 1930s and 1940s, against the professed wish of the British Mandate administration.

Of even greater importance is the functional nature of the settlements. An agricultural village is able to bring far more extensive tracts of land under control than a commuter or dormitory settlement. The area of land needed for farming is much larger than that taken up by residential buildings in commuter settlements. It is also often argued that the very essence of farming results in the forgeing of a stronger bond between the settler and the land – hence the sense of belonging to the area and the desire to retain ultimate control. A commuter simply lives in the area but spends the greater part of each day in distant towns and cities.

Certainly, settlement has always been used by Israeli governments (of whatever political colour) as a means of expressing their attachment to specific regions and of demonstrating their intent to retain ultimate territorial control. Such policies are a consequence in part of an ideological imperative: a major component of Zionism was the desire to 'return to the land' and to the agricultural origins of the Jewish people. But settlement dispersion was also a major factor in defining the ultimate borders of the state of Israel in 1948/49 (Fig 1.1). With the exception of one small region to the south of Jerusalem, none of the West Bank had previously been settled by the Zionist enterprise. This rocky upland region lacked the necessary resources for extensive agricultural cultivation. By contrast, the vast, empty, Negev desert region was included within the state's boundaries because it was perceived as constituting the future development region for new settlement projects.

Table 4.1: Growth of West Bank Jewish settler population

Year	Total	Increase	% increase
1976	3,176	—	—
1979	10,000	6,824	214.86
1982	21,000	11,000	110.00
1987	67,000	46,000	219.04

Source: Adapted from Benvenisti and Khayat (1988).

Settlement in the occupied territories

Despite the great geographical differences to be found within the West Bank, policies aimed at bringing the region (or part of it) under Israeli control following the 1967 War were still based around the settlement/colonisation concept. Between 1967 and 1989, some 118 new rural and urban settlements, containing approximately 70,000 people, were established throughout the West Bank and Gaza Strip (Table 4.1). In addition, a further 100,000 persons were resident in the new suburbs of East, South and North Jerusalem, all located beyond the previous 'green line' boundary (see Chapter 6). While the settlements are dispersed throughout the region, there is a clear concentration in the western margins of the West Bank in closest proximity to the old 'green line' boundary and the Israeli metropolitan centres, as well as in the immediate vicinity of Jerusalem (Fig 4.1). In addition, the Golan Heights has also been the subject of intensive colonisation by approximately 30 agricultural villages, aimed at

bolstering Israeli control over this peripheral, but strategically important, region along the border between Israel and Syria.

The colonisation process undertaken by the Israeli government has not been uniform throughout the past twenty years. The specific location of the settlements, and the pace of development, have fluctuated over time in line with changing Israeli government policy. The settlement process can be divided into four major periods: 1967–77; 1977–81; 1981–84; 1984 until the present time.

1967–77
The period between 1967 and 1977 was characterised by settlement policies carried out by the ruling Labour government and along the lines of the Allon Plan (Fig 4.2). The idea behind this policy was to ensure defensible borders on the one

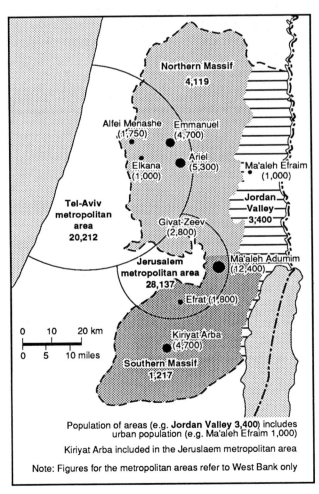

Population of areas (e.g. **Jordan Valley 3,400**) includes urban population (e.g. Ma'aleh Efraim 1,000)

Kiriyat Arba included in the Jeruslaem metropolitan area

Note: Figures for the metropolitan areas refer to West Bank only

Figure 4.1   Distribution of West Bank Jewish settlers, 1986
Source: Benvenisti and Khayat (1988).

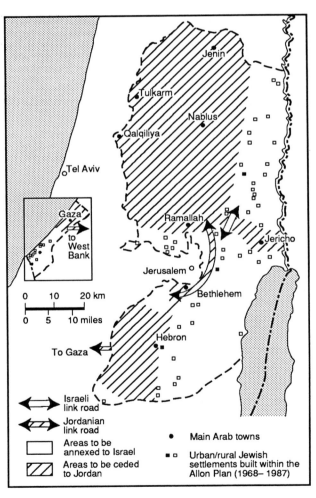

Figure 4.2   The Allon Settlement Plan
Note the proposed territorial corridor linking the autonomous Palestinian area with the state of Jordan. Jewish colonisation would take place mainly along the eastern boundary.
Source: Benvenisti and Khayat (1988).

Plates 1 and 2 show classic suburban forms of Jewish colonisation in the West Bank. Large detached houses, most sporting red-tiled roofs, are typical of these settlements. The appearance of these villages provides a striking contrast with the gentle slopes of the Western Samaria region (Plate 1) and with the local Arab villages and towns which blend in more readily to the local landscape. In Plate 2, the suburban villas of the Jewish settlers stand out in contrast to the narrow agricultural land plots belonging to local Palestinian inhabitants.

hand while at the same time leaving the interior of the West Bank empty of Jewish settlements. The intention was that this latter area could eventually become an autonomous Palestinian region with both territorial and functional links to the state of Jordan. Israel would nevertheless retain control of approximately 40 per cent of the West Bank land area and would insist on posting troops along the proposed border formed by the River Jordan. Two parallel north-south lines of agricultural settlements would be established along the Jordan Valley and the overlooking mountain slopes – the latter acting as a second line of defence (should the settlements at the bottom of the valley be overrun) as well as an early-warning station for military activities across the Jordan border. The small agricultural villages attracted relatively few settlers, but enabled extensive regional territorial control by means of widespread agricultural cultivation. Between 1967 and 1977, some 17 Israeli settlements were established along the Jordan Valley, housing a settler population of approximately 3,000 people. During the next ten years, the Allon Plan settlements stagnated, while some even underwent relative decline – both economically and demographically.

1977–81
The most significant change with respect to government policy on colonisation came about with the rise to power of the right-wing Likud government of Menahem Begin in 1977. This government rejected any notion of territorial concessions in the West Bank or, as they called the region, Judea and Samaria (see Table 2.1). The Likud administration promoted widespread settlement throughout the region as a means of

ensuring control of the territory. Unlike the previous Labour administrations, the Likud focused on settling the mountain ridge, the most densely populated area of Palestinian habitation, avoided by the Allon Plan. The creation of settlements in and around the territory densely populated by the indigenous inhabitants was meant to demonstrate the new government's resolve to retain the whole region under Israeli control.

Between 1977 and 1981, most settlement activity was initiated and implemented by the religious-nationalist movement, Gush Emunim. This movement had been formed in 1974, in the wake of the October 1973 War (see Table 1.1), in order to oppose any attempt by the Israeli governments to negotiate territorial concessions in the West Bank. Basing their claim to the region on the 'Divine' granting of the area to the Jewish people for eternity (see above, Chapter 2), they initially attempted to establish settlements in locations opposed by the then Labour government. With the coming to power of a hard-line government, the Gush Emunim movement was transformed from an ex-parliamentary protest group into the informal arm of implementation of a widespread colonisation policy (Fig 4.3).

This period also witnessed the founding of a new type of small settlement, known as the *Yshuv Kehillati* – or community village. Unlike the classic agricultural collectives, such as the *kibbutzim* and *moshavim* which dotted the Israeli rural landscape, the community settlements were mostly dormitory villages located within reasonable commuting distance of the major Israeli metropolitan centres of Tel Aviv and

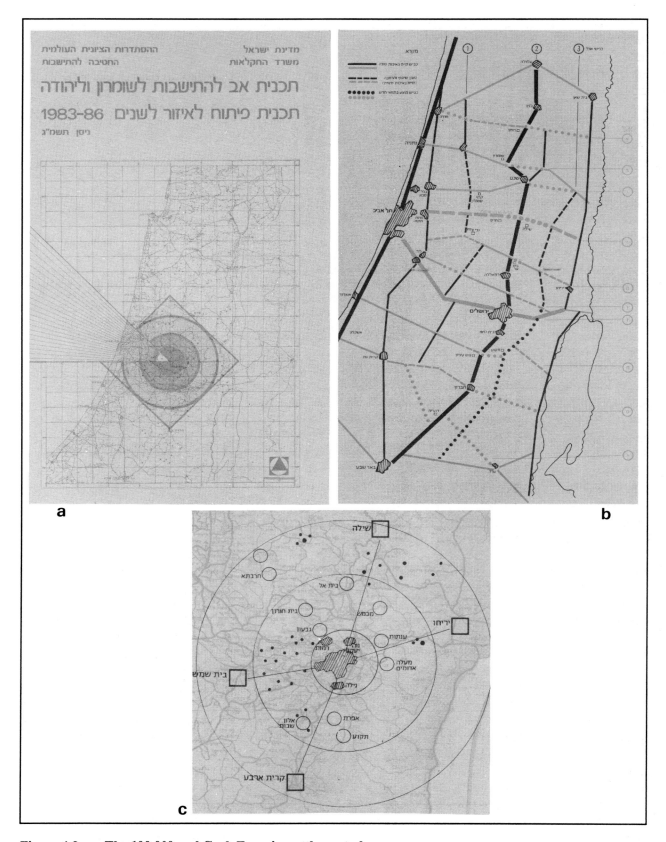

Figure 4.3 **The 100,000 and Gush Emunim settlement plans**

a) The cover of the 100,000 Plan (produced in 1983) depicting the West Bank as the metropolitan extension of Tel Aviv.

b) The Gush Emunim Plan (produced in 1978) proposed an extensive plan of road construction, linking the major Israeli cities in the coastal plain to the West Bank, thus facilitating easier transportation.

c) The extension of Jerusalem's metropolitan influence into the West Bank, as put forward in the Gush Emunim Plan.

Jerusalem. The potential settlers were not obliged to change their workplaces or to renounce family independence in favour of community decision-making. They were simply required to change their place of residence, in most cases exchanging a medium-sized apartment in town for a private detached house and a small plot of land within a 30–40 km radius of the city. Government incentives such as cheap land and large mortgages made the move a worthwhile proposition for most households considering relocating over the 'green line'.

Between 1977 and 1981, approximately 50 new settlements were established in the West Bank, adding approximately 11,000 people to the settler population.

1981–84

Under the second Likud government, between 1981 and 1984 the pace of development underwent a rapid increase, although the overall political objectives remained much the same as during the previous four years. The government opened up settlement to all groups who were prepared to become involved in the purchase of lands, development of infrastructure and the formation of an organisational structure for the individual settlement unit. In this way they removed the monopoly control of settlement implementation from the Gush Emunim and other, more bureaucratic, organisations. Policy-makers began to understand that, in order to attract a mass movement of settlers to the West Bank, it was important to play directly on the social and economic benefits to be had from such a move, rather than emphasising the ideological factors – an argument which appealed only to a diehard minority.

This more broadly-based approach to policy lay behind the '100,000 Settlement Blueprint' produced by a combination of government agencies in the early 1980s. The objective of this plan was to increase the West Bank Jewish settler population to 100,000 by the end of the decade. Advertising campaigns marketed the idea of private housing for the price of an apartment in the city, within 'commuting distance' of the previous workplaces and with all the 'quality of life' to be had from living in a small, quiet, green, village community (Figs 4.4, 4.5). Emphasis was placed on the area nearest to the old 'green line' boundary and the Israeli metropolitan centres, in an attempt to attract as many people in as short a time as possible. Many Israelis, not opposed to the

government settlement policy but at the same time not sufficiently motivated to relocate under difficult conditions (during the earlier period, settlers had often been obliged to live for long periods of time in temporary caravans without adequate electricity and water supplies), made the move. Between 1981 and 1984, a further 30 settlements were founded in the West Bank, and the total settler population increased to approximately 44,000. 1984 was itself a peak year for the arrival of new settlers, with over 16,000 being added to the West Bank Jewish population.

Most of the Gaza Strip settlements were established during this latter period, although the first villages were set up prior to 1981. The Labour government was opposed to the establishment of settlements in this densely populated, narrow coastal strip. Furthermore, a group of Jewish agricultural settlements already existed in the Yamit region of northern Sinai, directly to the south of the Gaza Strip. Under the Camp David Peace Accords, the Yamit settlements were evacuated and eventually razed. One of the immediate policy responses was to strengthen and expand the Gaza Strip settlements. By 1990, there were 16 Jewish communities in the southern section of the Gaza Strip, housing approximately 3,500 inhabitants.

1984 until the present

The fourth period was characterised by the consolidation of the existing colonisation network, with only a few additional settlements being established. This arose out of the paralysis affecting any West Bank policy following the formation of a National Unity government in the wake of the political stalemate at the 1984 elections. The right-wing Likud and left-wing Labour parties were equal partners in the new government. Labour demanded a curb on all further settlement activity as a condition for their entering the coalition government. For their part, the Likud agreed to accept a maximum of six new settlements.

While the groups favouring further colonisation – especially the Gush Emunim movement – vehemently opposed the virtual cessation of new settlement activity, it did enable them to consolidate the existing framework, much of which had been characterised by small communities lacking the necessary threshold for the provision of many basic services. Thus the settler population continued to increase annually, mostly through the consolidation and extension of

Dear Reader,

This publication is intended to present a full, factual perspective on the possibilities of coming to live in Judaea, Samaria, and the Gaza area.

Less than a decade ago, the establishment of new communities in Judaea, Samaria, and Gaza conjured up images of tents and portable generators, of official indifference, if not outright opposition. Unyielding idealism and spirited political debate were the characteristics of the reborn Jewish presence in the heart of the Land of Israel. Yet day after day, month after month, the presence grew, the few became many, until today, the facts on the ground have been translated into a new reality, both in terms of the nation's security and future development.

A majority of Israel has come around to the early settlers' bedrock vision and conviction that Judaea, Samaria, and Gaza are not some distant, foreign tracts, but rather an inseparable part of Israel, steeped in historic meaning and contemporary quality living.

Judaea, magnificent hills and Biblical landscape, is not "way out there" somewhere — at its closest point, it is about ½ mile from Jerusalem, the capital of Israel. Indeed Jerusalem is the historic Judaean city, the center of Judaean activity. So too, the green, rolling knolls of Samaria are only a 15-minute car ride, or less, from Netanya, Kfar Saba, Petach Tikva and the heart of Tel Aviv.

As Israelis by the tens of thousands reclaim the high lands which overlook the coastal plain, build anew where their forefathers built, dwell again where the prophets roamed, they are being joined by ever increasing ranks of newcomers, 'olim.' Jews from around the world have been drawn by new opportunities presented in Judaea, Samaria, and Gaza. Aliyah can be not only a relocation to cosmopolitan Tel Aviv or to any of Israel's other major cities, it can be another alternative. This is an opportunity to pioneer a new-old land and replant Jewish roots with one's own hands.

Judaea, Samaria and Gaza are beckoning, and Jews from all four corners of the globe are returning home. They are finding a scenario which stirs the imagination with its varieties of options and possibilities. A multiplicity of lifestyles is the rule, not the exception in these areas, experimentation thriving alongside tradition. Different kinds of communities are being formed, some guided more by the collective will, others completely wide-open towns in the spirit of Western individualism. Religious norms predominate in some communities, in others not — and in some, unique for Israeli society, the two co-exist in beautiful harmony.

Pragmatism and pioneering are the twin elements which spur on the exciting development of Judaea, Samaria, and Gaza today. The hillsides are blossoming. The children are thriving. The congregations are worshipping. The people of Israel are home . . . **really home** . . . once again.

WHO IS THE TYPICAL YISHUV RESIDENT?

In all fairness, average *yishuv-niks* are married couples in their 30's who have at least a few children. But having stated that reality, one must acknowledge the abundance of non-typical residents. Singles fit in particularly well in a yishuv ironi, or regular town, or in a completely new settlement being created with a high percentage of other singles. Persons over 40 years old might certainly be attracted to the high quality of life and placid surroundings of one of these communities, although they would probably be out of place at one of the youth movement yishuvim just getting under way. The bottom line is that there is something to please all kinds of people . . . if being in Judaea, Samaria, and Gaza is an important factor in one's personal objectives, then a suitable framework to accomodate that need can be found.

IS LIVING IN JUDAEA, SAMARIA, AND GAZA EXPENSIVE?

Some things are exceptionally reasonable. A two-storey private house, with a number of special flourishes, can be built for as little as $60,000-$75,000. For that sum in Tel Aviv, a modest three-room condominium might be found. Land development is also less expensive. Numerous tax breaks are given to residents of development areas and as mentioned previously, bank loans are available on favorable terms.

Some things such as gas, water, electricity and telephone service cost about the same all over Israel.

And some items do cost nominally more, such as groceries purchased in the communal store. One obviously has to make allowances for transport costs. Daily costs in Judaea, Samaria, and Gaza compare well with costs in more developed areas. All in all, fiscal advantages outweigh any disadvantages.

THIS GENERATION'S CHALLENGE: A STEP BY STEP GUIDE

Every generation of Jews confronts one central challenge, it is said. During the Twentieth Century, the enormous ramifications of both the Holocaust and the rebirth of the State of Israel obviously posed the chief confrontation to a coherent definition of Jewish existence. The individual Jew's response to genocide of his people was to forge a new bastion of Jewish strength from the ashes of Europe in the Land of Israel.

Today it can well be argued that return to Israel poses the paramount challenge — and opportunity — to the historic Jewish experience. Religious observance, Jewish education, aliyah are what the Jewish experience is all about. But in terms of the Historic Moment, the Big Picture, resettlement of Jews in the heart of Israel, Judaea, Samaria, and Gaza, towers as this generation's challenge which shows all signs of charting a new course for our people in centuries to come. While the path has been clearly set by the pioneers who preceded you, there is much exciting work still to be done, What follows is a step-by-step guide to enable any Jew anywhere to play his role in meeting this new challenge.

Figure 4.4   Promoting settlement
These extracts have been selected from a booklet issued in English aimed at encouraging American Jews to emigrate to Israel and to live in the West Bank.

Yuval Gad Ltd, a member of the Koor group, famed for its high standard of building, is one of the largest builders in Israel. In Yuval-Gad's cottage suburbs, the most modern building techniques are utilized, assuring first rate construction. "Jerusalem Stone" covered external walls and arched windows are just some of the features you'll find at these Yuval - Gad sites.

Givon (Givat Ze'ev)
On the main road planned between the Plains and Jerusalem
is a beautiful town in the heart of the
Jerusalem Hills. Givon's (Givat Ze'ev) location enables families employed in the
Plain's to live in a new town, in beautiful surroundings,
with all the essential public facilities.
Givon combines tranquillity and a young society, not far from Tel Aviv and Jerusalem.
A commercial centre serves the community,
including a Supermarket, Post Office, Bank, Health Services, synagogue, schools and Kindergardens.
Givon - a new start at an historical site.

Ma'aleh Adumim
Ma'aleh Adumim (8 km. East of Jerusalem) is a new and modern town, at a location that
assures a comfortable climate and spectacular view
(Jerusalem to the West and the Judean Desert and Dead Sea to the East).
Ma'aleh Adumim encorporates a complete system of public services.
- schools, kindergardens, synagogues, a cultural centre,
commercial centres, public parks, swimming pool and a stadium.

Details at the Jerusalem Yuval-Gad office.
Room 746, Clal Centre, 97 Jaffa Road, Jerusalem, Israel, Tel 02-234494 / 5.

YUVAL GAD LTD.

A HOME FOR YOU

*Kedumim (Samaria):
Hundreds of spacious
homes are being built in
Judea and Samaria,
cradle of the Kingdoms
of Judah and Israel.
The picture shows
archaeological remains
of the period of the
Israelite Monarchy
which overlook the
community settlement
Kedumim in Samaria.*

The Settlement Department of the World Zionist Organization has built a home for you.

YOU ARE INVITED TO COME TO SEE FOR YOURSELF THE
SCORES OF SETTLEMENTS ESTABLISHED IN
JUDEA AND SAMARIA AND THROUGHOUT THE LENGTH
AND BREADTH OF THE COUNTRY.
ACCEPT THE CHALLENGE OF BUILDING A NEW SETTLEMENT
AND CREATING A QUALITY OF LIVING
TO WHICH YOU ASPIRE.

MITZPE YEHUDA
THE GARDEN CITY

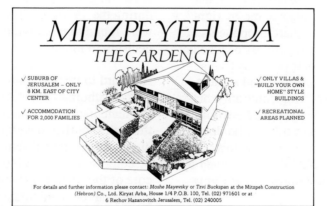

√ SUBURB OF JERUSALEM – ONLY 8 KM. EAST OF CITY CENTER

√ ACCOMMODATION FOR 2,000 FAMILIES

√ ONLY VILLAS & "BUILD YOUR OWN HOME" STYLE BUILDINGS

√ RECREATIONAL AREAS PLANNED

For details and further information please contact: Moshe Mayevsky or Tzvi Buckspan at the Mitzpeh Construction
(Hebron) Co., Ltd. Kiryat Arba, House 1/4 P.O.B. 100, Tel. (02) 971601 or at
6 Rechov Hazanovitch Jerusalem, Tel. (02) 240005

Figure 4.5   Colonising suburbia – settlement advertisements
The advertisements depicted here were aimed at attracting more settlers. The economic incentive of a detached house, at relatively cheap prices, is designed to appeal to new settlers who would not necessarily have gone to the West Bank for ideological reasons alone.

those settlements already established. Between 1984 and 1988, the Israeli settler population in the West Bank increased from 44,000 to 67,000 people.

Following the formation of a second broadly based coalition subsequent to the November 1988 elections, a similar agreement was reached concerning West Bank and Gaza settlement activity. Again, there were no constraints on the expansion and development of the existing settlements. However, the events of the Intifadeh

(the Palestinian uprising, see Chapter 7) and the fact that the major source of potential settlers had virtually dried up, has resulted in a slowing-down in the colonisation process. Excluding East Jerusalem and nine other 'urban' settlements, the size of many communities remained below 50 families per settlement. Not only were settlements competing with each other for the gradually dwindling settler potential; many were located in remote, inconvenient and unattractive locations for all but the most politically/ideologically orientated of settlers.

The process of suburban colonisation

Migration theory in general distinguishes between 'push' and 'pull' factors affecting the decision to move. The former reflect factors at the place of origin which cause a family to decide to leave, while the latter are factors which attract a person to a particular destination in preference to any other place. Within the Israeli context of settling the territories, we can broadly distinguish these two categories as 'quality of life' and 'ideology' respectively. Israeli towns are characterised by relatively high-density apartment blocks. There is little available land (at very high, unaffordable prices) for detached housing. Thus there has always been a desire on the part of many within the Israeli populace to leave the towns for more attractive surroundings. This 'push' factor has become transformed into a 'pull' factor by the attractive financial conditions offered by the government for the purchase of land plots and the construction of private housing within the West Bank.

An equally significant 'pull' factor is that of 'ideology', expressed as the belief that "I must settle the land because it belongs to me by right". Such a factor could attract diehard proponents of the 'Greater Israel' concept, regardless of whether or not they are improving their previous living conditions. Obviously, we will not find settlers who wish to improve their living conditions but are opposed to settling in the occupied territories. However, we may find many settlers who do not have strong political opinions for or against settling in the West Bank, but who are swayed by their desire substantially to improve their living conditions.

In a survey carried out by Juval Portugali and David Newman (1987) in the summer of 1985, over 700 West Bank Jewish settlers were interviewed about their motivations for having moved to the region. Of the respondents who answered this question, 47 per cent stated that they had moved for ideological reasons (i.e. they believed that it was necessary to settle the West Bank and thus retain Jewish/Israeli control over the region), a further 23 per cent stated that they had moved because of the expected 'quality of life' to be obtained in a low density, small, more rural community, while 17 per cent responded that they had been influenced by the 'low house price' as compared to the equivalent to be obtained in the Israeli metropolitan centres.

It is legitimate to assume that some respondents felt it necessary to give an ideologically 'positive' rather than a 'materialist' answer, although it is difficult to assess just how many. Thus the true percentage for the 'ideology' motivation is probably lower, while the 'quality of life' and 'low house price' motivations are correspondingly higher. It is worth noting, however, that when taking male and female responses separately, the male responses scored over 70 per cent on the 'ideology' motivation, while the women scored much higher on the 'quality of life' and 'low house price' motivations, relegating 'ideology' to third place.

In a further study carried out by Applebaum and Newman (1989) during the same period, survey material concerning the reasons for migration to new suburban settlements throughout Israel (not only the West Bank) was collected. While the general findings were similar to those described in the previous paragraph, the 'ideological' motivations scored considerably higher in the West Bank than they did in other regions, most notably the Galilee region. Although Galilee was a focus for politically sponsored settlement policies during the 1970s and 1980s - quality of life factors were found to be of major importance in the decision to move.

It is hard to imagine another case of what might be called 'suburban colonisation', i.e. the implementation of a political colonisation policy through suburban development. Clearly, the unique geographical setting, in which the area to be colonised was contiguous with the metropolitan core of the 'dominant' territory, enabled such policies to be manipulated in the pursuit of political objectives. Prior to 1967, the physical expansion of the Tel Aviv metropolitan region had been severely limited in terms of the direction it could take. To the east, the 'green line' boundary was a major physical obstacle, thus ensuring that most expansion took place north and south of the Tel Aviv core along the coastal plain.

Such a pattern of growth distorts the classic geographical models explaining urban residential expansion as an economic process. The greater the distance from the Central Business District (CBD), the cheaper will be the land. Thus business concerns take over the more expensive land near the centre, while residents seek cheaper land at the urban fringe. As a general rule, residents will seek the nearest available land and thus take advantage

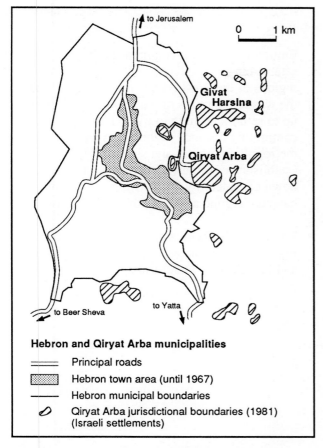

Figure 4.6   Jewish colonisation in Hebron
Starting from the urban suburb of Qiryat Arba, Jewish residential settlement around Hebron has spread in such a way as to limit the spontaneous expansion of the Arab town of Hebron towards the east.
Source: Romann (1985).

of the relatively cheap land price, within a reasonable distance (in terms of travelling time and cost) of the metropolitan core.

In the case of Israel prior to 1967, residential expansion took place at greater distances to the north and south of the city than was the case to the east, because the political boundary acted as an obstacle to further expansion. To a certain extent, the Israeli colonisation of the past twenty years has brought this 'natural' urban hinterland back into play. The development of roads such as the Trans-Samarian route linking the West Bank to the metropolitan core will further enhance the process of suburban colonisation.

Settlement in the urban context

One further aspect of settlement policy which must

be noted here concerns Jewish infiltration into Arab urban settlements. In addition to Jerusalem (see Chapter 6), Jewish colonisation has also taken place in the two major towns of Hebron and Nablus. In both cases the settler population is composed of religious ultra-nationalists who insist on maintaining a residence in these ancient biblical cities. In the case of Hebron, a Jewish presence did, in fact, continue to exist there until the 1920s and 1930s. Following the 1967 War, the Israeli government authorised the founding of a new Jewish suburb – Qiryat Arba – overlooking Hebron. Today Qiryat Arba houses a few thousand residents (Falah, 1985; Romann, 1985). From 1979, however, the settlers demanded a presence within the Arab town of Hebron itself resulting in the requisition and rehabilitation of a number of buildings which had previously been under Jewish ownership. This gave rise to direct confrontation and bitter violence between the two neighbouring, but mutually hostile, sets of inhabitants. Needless to say, the settler element within Hebron constitutes only a small minority of the total town population. However, the ultimate long-term plan calls for the physical linking of the Jewish 'neighbourhood' in the centre of the town with the large Qiryat Arba suburb, by means of a territorial corridor of unbroken Jewish residence (Fig 4.6).

As in all the five towns in Israel in which both Jews and Arabs reside, the two groups display almost total physical and residential segregation. While this may initially have been partially due to cultural and 'in-group' desires for segregation, it has become a simple necessity of life as tensions and violence increase. Jewish settlers in Hebron and parts of East Jerusalem are not free to walk about alone, or at least not without loaded firearms. Thus to a certain extent it could be argued that settlers in such places (and especially the women who remain at home during the day) have, paradoxically, become virtual prisoners within the neighbourhoods that they settled as a means to demonstrate their control. This phenomenon has increased as a result of the Intifadeh (see Chapter 7).

In concluding this chapter, it is important to note that although the region(s) at present undergoing intensive settlement are in direct physical proximity to Israel and constitute a territorial and physical extension of the state, social integration does not take place easily or quickly. This is the result of the political animosity displayed by each group for the other.

Summary

- Since 1967, Israeli governments have established civilian settlements throughout the West Bank as a means of ensuring long-term territorial control of the region.

- By 1990, approximately 70,000 Jewish settlers resided in the West Bank, and a further 70,000 lived in the urban suburbs which have been established around Jerusalem.

- Settlement colonisation underwent four major phases Between 1967 and 1977, it followed the minimalist policies of the ruling Labour party; from 1977 to 1981, the nationalist Gush Emunim movement commenced the establishment of villages within the upland regions of the West Bank; from 1981 to 1984, the western margins of the region were opened up to settlers wishing to live within commuting distance of the Tel Aviv metropolitan region; and since 1984, the establishment of new settlements has slowed down considerably but existing settlements have undergone a process of consolidation.

- There has also been a process of 'infiltration' into some urban areas, most notably Hebron and the Old City of Jerusalem.

5 Functional, social and territorial duality

Administrative duality

THE ADMINISTRATION OF BOTH the West Bank and Gaza Strip by Israel takes on a dual pattern. Notwithstanding the fact that the region constitutes a territorial extension of the state of Israel, the form of administration is different in the two regions – at least in so far as it applies to the Palestinian inhabitants. In the first place, the West Bank is considered as being 'occupied territory', and it has not been annexed by Israel (with the exception of East Jerusalem). Thus even the Israeli government is aware of the fact that under international law, full civilian rule cannot be extended to this region. The civilian administration is directly controlled by, and answerable to, the military authorities.

However, the Jewish settler population of the West Bank is administered according to one set of rules, while the Palestinians are subject to another. The only common feature is the dependence of both groups on the military government. Following the conquest of the region in 1967, the Israeli authorities divided the West Bank into seven sub-districts, based largely on the previous Jordanian divisions. The major exception to this pattern was the incorporation of East Jerusalem into the Israeli administrative framework (Fig 5.1). Moreover, Jordanian law still governs matters relating to purely civilian problems. During the 1970s, a civilian administration was set up, the idea being that local Palestinians should become more directly involved in the day-to-day running of local affairs. However, this was viewed by many Palestinians – especially the PLO – as a form of betrayal and collaboration. The state of Jordan continued to intervene directly (with Israel's approval) in local administrative affairs until King Hussein's public withdrawal in 1988, shortly before the PLO's declaration of an independent Palestinian state.

The Jewish settlements on the West Bank are administered according to the Israeli model of local government, based on a three-tier hierarchy. This ranges from full municipality status (for towns of over 20,000 inhabitants) through local council (for settlements ranging between 2,000 and 20,000 inhabitants), to the remaining small

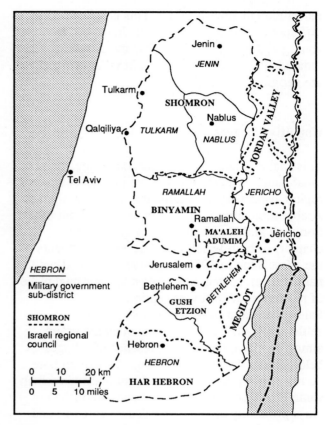

Figure 5.1 **Dual administrative regions in the West Bank**
The map shows the superimposition of Israeli regional council (rural municipalities) boundaries onto the existing Palestinian administrative divisions.
Source: Benvenisti and Khayat (1988).

villages which are incorporated within regional rural councils. The larger of the West Bank Jewish settlements have attained local council status, while the majority of the settlements have been incorporated into one of the six regional rural councils covering the West Bank territory (Fig 5.1). However, even here there is a distinction to be made between the operation of regional councils within the pre-1967 boundaries and those in the occupied territories. Within Israel proper, the jurisdictional area covered by the rural regional council covers all Jewish and Arab settlements which do not have independent local council or municipality status. Within the West Bank and Gaza Strip however, the regional councils comprise the Jewish settlements only. The Palestinian settlements are subject to an alternative form of administration organised by the military government. In other words, the same piece of territory is subject to a dual administrative system depending on a settlement's affiliation to the Palestinian or Jewish sector. This is reflected in differential policies of resource allocation, land zoning and granting of permits, and differences in judicial and economic systems in villages which are geographical neighbours.

Cognitive images

This spatial duality is strengthened by the inhabitants' respective cognitive images of the region, especially as regards the 'other' (Jewish or Arab) ethnic group. In the survey carried out by Portugali and Newman (1987, see previous chapter) of both Israeli and Palestinian residents of the West Bank in 1985, respondents were asked to name the ten settlements nearest to their own place of residence. With few exceptions, both Palestinians and Israelis mentioned only settlements affiliated to their own ethnic group, almost totally ignoring the presence of villages belonging to the opposing group. This often bore no relationship to the geographical reality in which some Israeli settlements have been established in close proximity to existing Palestinian towns and villages.

The same survey also observed the extent to which the residents of each settlement were prepared to undergo commercial and other interchange with settlements of the 'other' ethnic group. With few exceptions, both Palestinians and Israelis were found to operate within their own separate ethnic territories, further emphasising the separate functionality of the region and its inhabitants. Despite the fact that local markets or commercial centres are to be found in neighbouring Palestinian settlements, most of the Jewish residents preferred to do their shopping in Tel Aviv or other Jewish towns located at a far greater distance from their homes. This was due partly to a feeling of fear of entering the densely populated Palestinian settlements (a feeling which has intensified since the onset of the Intifadeh in 1987 – see Chapter 7) and partly because, before returning home of an evening, Jewish residents working in Jewish towns deal with any other necessary commercial activities, such as visiting a bank, a supermarket or a dentist.

Commuting patterns

The commuting patterns of both sets of inhabitants present a further aspect of this dual geography. Nearly all Israeli settlers and approximately 110,000 Palestinian residents commute daily from their homes in the West Bank and Gaza Strip to places of employment in the Israeli towns. They travel at the same time, in the same direction, on the same roads – many of which have been constructed or improved during the past ten years as a means of facilitating east-west links between the West Bank and Israel. Many of these roads have been constructed in such a way as to bypass the major Palestinian urban centres, thus leaving ethnic 'exclaves', through which the Israeli settlers do not travel. Palestinians and Israelis make use of their own private car pools or public transport. The local Palestinian public transport service is highly localised and fragmented, while the Israeli semi-national Egged bus company reaches all Jewish settlements but largely bypasses Arab localities.

When they reach their destination, the Israeli settlers go to their jobs, mostly in administration and management, while the Palestinians constitute a cheap source of immigrant labour in the urban centres, employed mostly in menial, blue-collar tasks. It is estimated that approximately 110,000 Palestinians from the West Bank and Gaza Strip work daily in the Israeli metropolitan centres. Official Israeli figures account for around 60–70,000 labourers, but recent surveys have suggested that this is an underestimate by at least a third. The official statistics cover only those workers who are formally registered with the labour authorities and who comply with the stringent legislation concerning their employment conditions. Both employers and employees benefit from informal, under-the-table transactions. For their part, Israeli employers are required to provide minimal social benefits to all registered employees and so they cut their costs by hiring temporary labour on a daily, or weekly, informal basis. Many employees prefer to remain overnight in poor, shack-like accommodation on building and work sites, rather than face the time and cost of daily journeys to and from the West Bank or Gaza. While this is forbidden under Israeli law, it is estimated that tens of thousands of people spend the week in insanitary and overcrowded conditions within the Israeli cities, especially in the Arab neighbourhood of Adjami in Jaffa which was an Arab town prior to 1948 and has since been incorporated into the city limits of Tel Aviv.

The most characteristic feature of the cheap-labour phenomenon are the daily 'labour markets' which have sprung up around major traffic intersections leading into the Israeli cities. From around 4.30 am, Palestinians seeking work tend to congregate at certain key locations in the hope that foremen requiring temporary labour – usually on building sites, or as fill-in gardeners and cleaners – will hire them. The bargaining process is carried out speedily; labour supply usually outstrips demand and so enables the payment of extremely low rates. Many Israeli public institutions rely on these labour markets to ensure a sufficient supply of menial labour. Employment-related problems, such as hiring, meals and accommodation (where necessary) are often dealt with by private agencies, in most cases taking as much per employee as they eventually pass on in wages. While the supply of Palestinian labour has decreased as a result of the Intifadeh, the process continues to operate.

This use of cheap labour is similar, in many respects, to the *gasterbeiter* phenomenon to be found in many European countries. But in the Israeli case, it is even more flexible. While many European countries take in cheap labour on a seasonal, or even annual, basis – after which they can send them back to their home countries if they are no longer required – in Israel much of the hiring is on a daily basis. The relative proximity of the labourers' home in the West Bank to the place of employment – at most an hour's journey – enables many Israeli employers to get the cheapest possible labour on the most temporary basis.

While some Palestinians have remained in fixed jobs over a relatively long period of time, they represent a minority of the total labour supply. Juval Portugali (1989) has pointed out that, in contrast to many Jewish menial workers, the 'nomad' Palestinian labour force displays great spatial flexibility and is not tied down to any one place of work. Such workers may even find themselves in a better position than that of the Israeli unemployed who are less prepared to travel great distances or give up on their social welfare benefits for the sake of a poorly paid job.

Economic duality and core-periphery relations

The nature of the relationships between Israel and the West Bank also takes on many other forms. Most important are the economic linkages which are dictated by the requirements of the Israeli capitalist economy. Within Israel, the processes of production and consumption are highly protected – to the benefit of the Israeli producer. This is applicable to both industry and agriculture, but especially the latter. The same regulations do not apply within the West Bank for Palestinian industrial or agricultural enterprises. Thus the Israeli producers are afraid that an influx of cheaper (in price, not necessarily in quality) goods from the occupied territories will severely damage their own profitability. As a result, Israel does not allow the free transfer of manufactured goods or agricultural produce from the territories into Israel – although it is to be assumed that there is always a certain amount of fruit and vegetables which manage to slip in to the Israeli markets. But local demand from the West Bank is insufficient to account for the local agricultural produce as supply far outstrips demand. Thus the Israeli government actively encourages the export of West Bank produce through the open bridges with Jordan and from there into the markets of the neighbouring Arab countries. This policy has been in operation since 1967.

Within the industrial sector, the West Bank suffers from under-development. Again owing to fears on the part of the Israeli producer that cheap goods will flow into the highly protected – and hence expensive – Israeli shops, the Israeli administration has not encouraged investment in industrial infrastructure in the West Bank. On the contrary, many of the large Israeli manufacturers find outlets for their surplus goods in the Palestinian markets and commercial centres – often at a cheaper price than within Israel itself!

For those students familiar with the core-periphery model of colonial relations, in which the core (in this case Israel) is able to manipulate the periphery (the West Bank and Gaza Strip) to its own benefit, this is a classic case study, albeit on a small scale. A dual economy has grown up, with the modern, advanced enterprises and services being located within the core and the less advanced, more traditional economy, in the periphery. It is the lack of an industrial base which is probably the most serious disadavantage facing any future independent or autonomous region within the West Bank.

Thus duality and segregation pervade all aspects of daily life in the relationships between Israelis and Palestinians. The specific nature of the duality is a function of the degree of economic dependency each group has for the other. Territory and economy have become increasingly intertwined in a complex set of relationships. Yet because of the dominant-subordinate and majority-minority nature of the segregation, little constructive contact takes place between the two national groups occupying the same territory. It is to be expected that under such conditions, the formation of attitudes by each group for the other will continue to be based on mutual antagonism and will serve only to further intensify the political conflict.

Summary

- The West Bank and Gaza Strip are administered according to a dual system of control, with separate administrative divisions of the region.

- Jewish settlers are subject to Israeli law, while Palestinians are subject to Jordanian law, both administered through the Israeli military authorities.

- Both Israelis and Palestinians commute from their homes in the West Bank to their places of work in the major Israeli cities. While the Israelis fill mostly managerial and other white-collar jobs, the Palestinians make up the cheap, menial labour force of the large cities.

- Both Israelis and Palestinians view the West Bank only in terms of their own ethnic group. In their daily activities, each tends to ignore the existence of settlements belonging to the other group.

6 Jerusalem

WITHIN THE WIDER CONTEXT of the occupied
territories, the case of Jerusalem requires separate
attention. Nothing arouses more intense debate and
conflict than the question of 'who will control' the
holy city – holy to Judaism, Islam and
Christianity. For Jews – and hence modern Israelis
– Jerusalem is the site of the ancient Jewish
temples, the remains of which provide an
emotional focus for Jews worldwide. For Muslims,
Jerusalem is the third most holy site (after Mecca
and Medina), containing the El Aqsa and Dome of
the Rock mosques (Plate 1). For Christians,
Jerusalem is the site of Jesus's last meal and his
subsequent resurrection, and contains the stations
of the cross to which the faithful flock each year.

Under the British Mandate, free access was
provided for members of all faiths to the holy
sites. Jerusalem was declared the capital city of
Israel soon after the declaration of the state in
1948, despite the fact that the undisputed
economic – and for a time political – centre was
Tel Aviv. As a result of the hostilities between
Israel and Jordan during 1948, the city was
physically divided between an Eastern Arab
(Jordanian) sector and a Western (Israeli) sector.
From 1948 to 1967, access to Jewish Jerusalem
was limited to a single territorial corridor running
from the coastal plain to the west of the city (Fig
6.1). The physical division of the city meant that
the holy sites of all faiths located in the Old City
were under Jordanian rule – with no Jewish access
– while the residents of the Jewish Quarter were
evacuated to West Jerusalem.

Immediately following the conquest of Jerusalem
in 1967, Israel passed a law in the Knesset (Israeli
Parliament) formally annexing the eastern section
of the city and declaring a united Jerusalem as its
eternal capital (Fig 6.2). While the extension of
civilian law to the eastern sector has never been
recognised by any international forum, Israel sees
itself as the legitimate sovereign throughout the
urban area. Civilian rights (including the right to
vote in local, but not national elections) have been
formally extended to the Palestinian inhabitants of
East Jerusalem. They have, however, been
steadfast in their refusal to take up this offer.
While Israel views a united Jerusalem as its
capital, never again to be divided, the Palestinians
see East Jerusalem as the future centre of their
own independent state. All municipal policy

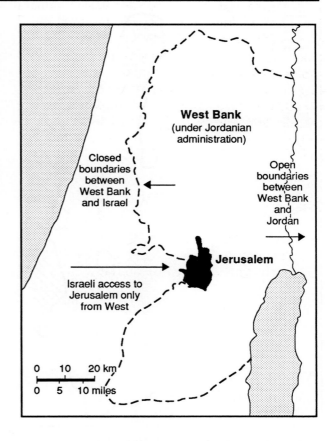

Figure 6.1   Location of Jerusalem, 1948–67
Until 1967, access to West Jerusalem was
limited to a territorial corridor running
from Jerusalem itself to the coastal plain
in the west. This corridor was bolstered
by much military and settlement activity
in order to prevent it being cut off in any
future war.

undertaken since 1967 has perceived the whole
Jerusalem area as a single city and many important
infrastructural networks have been combined.

The Old City of Jerusalem remains unique within
the urban fabric. Until 1967, the walls of the city
constituted a physical boundary between the
Jordanian- and Israeli-controlled sectors (Plate 2).
In periods of heightened tension, the walls
provided a cover for Jordanian sniping into the
western sector. Following the capture of the Old
City in 1967, the area around Judaism's most holy
site, the Western (Wailing) Wall, was cleared so as
to enable Jewish worshippers to visit. The Muslim
and Christian holy sites were placed under the
daily administration and management of their own
respective religious leaders, albeit within the
framework of overall Israeli control of the city.

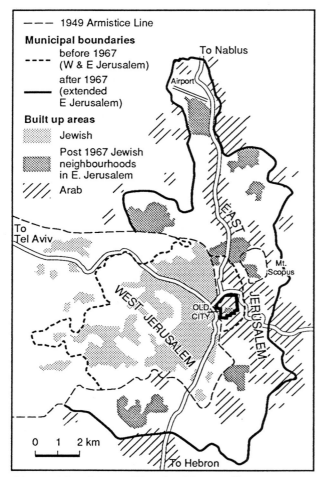

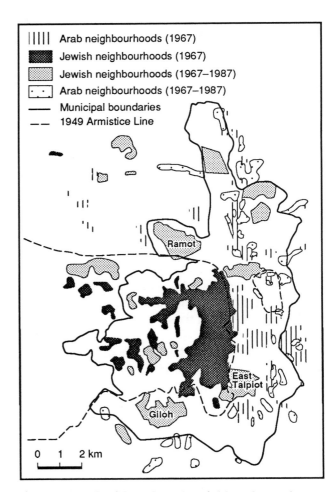

Figure 6.2 **Master Plan for Metropolitan Jerusalem, 1982**
Following the capture of East Jerusalem in 1967, the Israeli government annexed the newly gained areas and declared a 'united Jerusalem'. The new municipal boundaries were delimited in such a way as to maximise the territorial extent and the Jewish population, while minimising the Palestinian presence within the jurisdictional area.
Source: Benvenisti and Khayat (1988).

Figure 6.3 **Jewish and Arab neighbourhoods in Jerusalem, 1983**
After 1967, the Israeli government embarked upon a project of constructing massive Jewish urban neighbourhoods in the north, south and east of Jerusalem. These new neighbourhoods (with over 70,000 residents in the mid-1980s) were founded as a means of proclaiming Jewish sovereignty over the whole of the city and in order to prevent any future possibility of repartition.

Physical change in a 'united' city:

As a means of establishing control over the whole city, the Israeli government has undertaken a process of massive urban development in areas which were previously located beyond the dividing line. Whereas prior to 1967 expansion of the city took place only to the west, urban growth – in the form of large new neighbourhoods – has since taken place to the north, south and east. Over 70,000 Israelis now reside in these new neighbourhoods, the majority in the three large urban developments of Ramot, Giloh and East Talpiot (Fig 6.3). The implications of such development are twofold. First, the establishment of these neighbourhoods is a way of demonstrating

the supposed 'indivisibility' of the city in such a way that Arab and Jewish neighbourhoods – although remaining physically segregated – are enfolded within each other throughout the urban area. Secondly, the spread of neighbourhoods to the north, east and south of the city provides Jewish Jerusalem with a larger territorial buffer than that previously provided by the single land corridor to the west.

Prominent amongst the frenzied building activity has been the reconstruction of the university and hospital complexes on Mount Scopus in the north of the city, in what had remained a small Israeli exclave during 1948–67. Additional settlements have been established outside the Jerusalem

Plate 1. Arab and Jewish holy sites in close proximity in the heart of the Old City of Jerusalem. The Western (Wailing) Wall – a remnant of the ancient Jewish Temples – is the major focus for Jews, while the Dome of the Rock is one of the two important mosques (the other is the El Aqsa Mosque) for Muslim worshippers. On the horizon can be seen the vast university, hospital and housing complex on Mount Scopus, which was constructed after 1967 in the north of the city. On October 8th 1990, stones were thrown on to Jewish worshippers at the Western Wall from above. In the bloody sequel, 21 Palestinians were killed and many injured.

municipal boundaries but within the wider urban area. This has led to an interesting conflict of interests between Israeli policy-makers. The

government argues that it is important to establish these peripheral settlements in order to ensure territorial presence and control throughout the wider Jerusalem region and thus create a buffer between the expanding Arab settlements in the vicinity. By contrast, Jerusalem Mayor Teddy Kollek has opposed this policy on the grounds that the new suburban settlements draw the Jewish population out of the city itself, thus weakening the Jewish : Palestinian population balance within the municipal boundaries.

Both Jews and Arabs commute from their respective homes to their workplaces within the city, resulting in Jerusalem becoming dependent on its metropolitan hinterland. Existing roads have been widened and new roads have been constructed as a means of securing access to and from Jerusalem in all directions. There has also been a concerted attempt on the part of the right-wing Likud administrations to construct a new government centre in East Jerusalem to which a number of major ministries have moved their offices.

The Old City has also experienced major physical change with the renovation of the Jewish Quarter into a residential neighbourhood and the clearing of Arab residences in the proximity of the Western Wall. The latter area has been transformed from a religious focus to one that witnesses many state ceremonies – thus enhancing claims of sovereignty – throughout the year. During the past few years, more extreme nationalist elements have also begun to penetrate into parts of the Muslim Quarter, leading to heightened tension and violence between the two groups. The street markets of the Arab Quarter (*souks*) were a major attraction for tourists and local residents alike until the recent onset of the Intifadeh resulted in a major fall-off in trade.

Table 6.1 Growth of population in Jerusalem, 1967–88 (000s)

Year	Total	Jews	%	Non-Jews	%
1967	267.8	196.5	73.3	71.3	26.7
1972	313.8	230.3	73.3	83.5	26.7
1976	366.3	266.0	72.6	100.3	27.4
1980	407.1	292.3	71.7	114.8	28.2
1984	447.8	321.1	71.6	126.5	28.4
1988	493.5	353.9	71.7	139.6	28.3

Source: *Jerusalem Statistical Yearbook:*
No. 3, 1983, Table III/1, p.22.
No. 7, 1988, Table III/1, p.26.

Plate 2. The boundary between East and West Jerusalem prior to 1967 partially followed the walls of the Old City. To the right of the picture can be seen part of the walls, beyond which are the roofs of religious institutions (mostly Christian) in the Old City itself. To the left can be seen high-rise apartment blocks which were previously in West Jerusalem and which are now being cleared for a modern commercial and luxury housing development linking the west (Jewish) with the east (Arab) parts of the city. The previous no-man's land has been developed as a major traffic artery running from north to south, surrounded by parkland. On a calm day, it is hard to imagine that this picturesque scene is the focus for one of the world's most bitter conflicts.

In the spring of 1990, a group of nationalist Jewish settlers moved into a building in the Muslim Quarter of the Old City. The building, previously the property of the Greek Orthodox Church, had been purchased by a Panamanian organisation acting as a cover for the settlers. Following the immediate outcry on the part of both local Palestinian residents and the Church (who contested the legality of the sale) the Israeli High Court ordered the settlers to evacuate the building pending a full investigation of the affair. However, this incident brought to over twenty the number of buildings purchased and renovated by Jewish settlers as a means of expanding their presence throughout the Old City (Fig 6.4). While the purchase of some, if not all, of these buildings may have been carried out legally, the provocative nature of such activities within such a tense political atmosphere cannot be ignored.

Division within unity: human activity patterns

Despite the overall Jewish majority within the Jerusalem municipal area, natural increase amongst the Jewish population is only about half of the Arab increase, with the latter having doubled between 1967 and 1985 (Table 6.1).

Immediately following unification in 1967, the demographic balance was 73 per cent Jews and 27 per cent Arabs. This had changed to 71.6 per cent and 28.4 per cent respectively by 1985. In order to maintain the present ratio between Jews and Arabs within the city, the Jewish population must increase by approximately 3.7 per cent per annum. But low natural increase, and a recent tendency for limited outmigration of Jewish residents of the city – either to the new surrounding settlements or to the Tel Aviv region – suggest that the demographic balance will continue to work (albeit slowly) in favour of the Palestinians.

One of the major factors contributing to Jewish outmigration from the city is the fact that many Jewish residents perceive the city as being taken over by the growing power of ultra-religious Jewish groups. Unlike the remainder of the Jewish population, the ultra-religious groups experience extremely high natural increase – on a par with the Palestinian growth rates. They see Jerusalem as a 'holy' city and attempt to use their political power (seats in the Jerusalem municipality) to block all forms of development which may be interpreted as contributing to the 'secularisation' of the city. In response, many non-orthodox Jews prefer to migrate to the largely secular cities of the coastal plain.

Some of the ultra-religious groups (albeit a minority) profess an anti-Zionist ideology and do not recognise the legitimacy of a secular Jewish state. Jerusalem Mayor Teddy Kollek is on record as stating his fears that a coalition between these ultra-religious Jews and the East Jerusalem Palestinian vote (were they all to participate in the electoral process) could, in the near future, bring a non-Zionist city government to power. It is, therefore, to the advantage of the government that the East Jerusalem Palestinians have opted not to exercise the civilian – and hence voting – powers given to them by the Israeli government following its annexation of the city.

Since his initial victory in the mid-1960s, Mayor Kollek has continued successfully to contest all city elections although his independent 'One Jerusalem' party is closely identified with the Labour Party. Owing to his strong personality, Kollek has succeeded in drawing support from across the political spectrum. But Kollek is over seventy and likely to step down soon. In such an eventuality, it is likely that city contested elections will revert to the battle between right and left which is so typical in nearly all other Israeli cities,

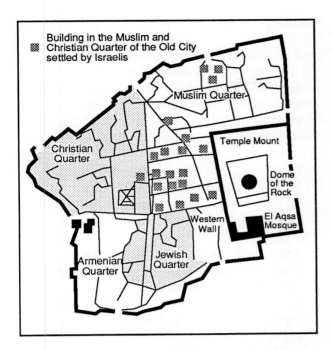

Figure 6.4   Jewish settlement in the Old City of Jerusalem
Jewish settlement has gradually spread outwards from the Jewish Quarter into the Muslim Quarter. This has been carried out by the purchase of buildings in an *ad hoc* fashion.

and which tend to mirror the national political divisions. Based on the evidence of national election results in Jerusalem, the right-wing Likud party could obtain a majority in the Jerusalem municipality. The implications for such a scenario would be a heightening of tensions between Arab and Jew throughout the city.

It is clear that the physical unification of the city has not brought about any meaningful human

contact between Jewish and Arab residents, over and beyond the manager-worker, or dominant-subordinate relations described in the previous chapter. With few exceptions, neighbourhoods remain highly segregated – Jewish neighbourhoods in the west, Arab neighbourhoods in the east of the city. There have hardly been any cases of Jews wishing to live in East Jerusalem Arab neighbourhoods (excluding the Old City, where the spread of Jewish residences is politically motivated), while any attempt by Arab residents to purchase cheap apartments in Jewish neighbourhoods is usually met by opposition on the part of local residents.

In an interesting study of schoolchildren from both West and East Jerusalem, geographer Michael Romann has demonstrated that Jewish and Arab teenagers rarely visit the 'other' side of the city and this is expressed in their lack of spatial knowledge when crossing the invisible dividing line. Residents of East Jerusalem are more dependent on West Jerusalem – owing to the concentration of government offices and employment opportunities in the Jewish sector – than are West Jerusalemites on East Jerusalem. As a result, Palestinians have a better grasp of Hebrew than do Israelis of Arabic. But residents of East Jerusalem are often subject to road-blocks and document checks when in West Jerusalem, resulting in their reluctance to visit that sector. For their part, Israeli residents of West Jerusalem have become increasingly frightened of being attacked when in East Jerusalem, and they too have mostly ceased travelling to the 'other' side, be it to visit tourist sites or to purchase cheaper goods in the Arab shops.

*New Israeli suburbs have been constructed beyond the 'green line' as part of a Greater Jerusalem. **Plate 3** shows the suburb of Giloh to the south of the city. Most housing consists of high-rise, high-density, apartment blocks covered by Jerusalem stone. **Plate 4** shows the large Ramot suburb to the north of Jerusalem, while in the immediate foreground are the remnants of an Arab village which occupied this spot. Running from south to north is a new highway, one of many constructed during the past ten years as a series of by pass routes aimed at linking the old and new neighbourhoods in a single functional unit.*

44

The future of Jerusalem?

The declared intent of all Israeli governments, whatever their political persuasion, that Jerusalem remain united under Israeli sovereignty, is a major obstacle to the Israeli proposal to hold elections in the West Bank. Many Israeli leaders are of the opinion that the election proposal applies to the West Bank excluding Jerusalem and its inhabitants; Jerusalem – in their opinion – forms part of the sovereign State of Israel. Others – including most world leaders – are of the the opinion that the elections should be open to all West Bank residents, including the inhabitants of East Jerusalem.

Outside Israel, the most commonly-heard solution for Jerusalem is some form of international control, allowing free and equal access to the holy sites of all three major monotheistic religions – Christianity, Islam and Judaism. But this is rejected by Israelis and Palestinians, both of whom demand sovereignty over the city. The Mayor of Jerusalem, Teddy Kollek, has occasionally suggested a system of neighbourhood councils, or boroughs, in which the Jewish and Arab neighbourhoods would have a certain level of self-government, but would remain under ultimate Israeli sovereignty. Palestinians demand the repartition of the city into two separate sovereign entities. This latter proposal would be all the more difficult to implement owing to the gradual, but continuous, integration of the physical infrastructure and service delivery systems of both parts of the city by the Jerusalem municipality.

Summary

• Following the capture of East Jerusalem in 1967, the city was formally reunified and annexed by the state of Israel. Thus, despite the lack of international recognition, Israel extends full state sovereignty – and hence civilian law – over East Jerusalem.

• East Jerusalem Palestinians do not accept Israel's claim to sovereignty over their neighbourhoods, and reject the offer of full citizenship.

• Since 1967, the Israeli government has established major urban suburbs in the north, east and south of Jerusalem (beyond the former 'green line' boundary) as a means to consolidate their control over an undivided city. Over 70,000 residents live in these neighbourhoods (1988).

• Jerusalem Mayor Teddy Kollek has proposed a system of autonomous neighbourhood rule (under Israeli sovereignty) in an attempt to distribute power to all communities in a more equitable fashion.

• New Jewish settlements have also been established within the Jerusalem urban hinterland, but outside the municipal limits. Some Israeli officials argue that this is self-defeating as it draws Jewish residents out of the city and thus results in a closing demographic gap between Palestinian and Jewish residents.

7 The Intifadeh

DESPITE TWENTY YEARS of occupation from 1967, the basic set of relationships between a dominant power (Israel) and subordinate population (West Bank Palestinians) remained largely unchanged. Opposition to continued Israeli control of the region was, with some exceptions, reflected in acts of violence performed outside the West Bank and outside Israel altogether. Thus, while Israel was continually threatened by external Palestinian opposition, Israel's territorial hold over the West Bank remained unchallenged. The founding of civilian settlements on the one hand, and the daily flow of Palestinian labour into the Israeli cities on the other, brought about an increased territorial and economic interdependence of each group. Whilst Israeli settlers were dependent on the West Bank territory for their settlements and Israeli manufacturers were dependent on a cheap source of labour from the West Bank and Gaza, the Palestinians remained dependent on the Israeli economy for their source of livelihood.

Origins: action and reaction

With the onset of the Intifadeh (Palestinian uprising), these relationships have changed significantly. Starting from a seemingly minor traffic incident in the Gaza Strip in December 1987, the West Bank and Gaza Palestinians have openly challenged the Israeli military administration. Continuous demonstrations and acts of violence against the Israeli army and settlers, most notably the use of Molotov cocktails and stone throwing, resulted in a cycle of violence and fatalities throughout 1988 and into 1989. In addition, acts of civil disobedience, such as the disruption of commerce and public services, economic strikes, tax boycotts, and the intimidation, and sometimes murder, of those regarded as collaborators of Israel, (Curtis, 1988/89) have become effective.

The Israeli army, considered to be amongst the most effective fighting forces in the world, has been unable to control or put down the Intifadeh. Soldiers who have been trained to face tanks and armies have been transformed into policemen, charged with maintaining order amongst a highly charged civilian population. As the Intifadeh has continued, so the Israeli response has become increasingly strong-armed, with the widespread use of batons and plastic bullets. This has resulted in numerous fatalities, with 250 Palestinians having been killed by early 1988 and over 600 by 1989. Some thirty Israelis, some soldiers and others civilians, were also killed during this period. Intifadeh leaders have been deported, the West Bank school system was closed down for the better part of a year and attempts were made to restrict the flow of money to the West Bank from outside sources.

Within Israel, the reaction has been twofold. The hard-liners of the right-wing Likud party have argued for an even stronger policy aimed at suppressing the uprising, including the expulsion of agitators, the destruction of houses used by terrorists and their families and the widespread use of curfews. For their part, the centre and left of public opinion have come out in opposition to the use of such tactics which, they claim, are eating away at the moral fibre of Israeli society. The fact that the uprising has not been put down, despite the strong-arm tactics of the Israeli army, is used by the centre and left as an argument to demonstrate the futility of continued occupation and attempted control of over a million Palestinians. A small number of soldiers – some from the elite fighting units – have refused to undertake their reserve duty in the occupied territories and have preferred to spend extended periods of time in military prisons.

For their part, the Palestinians have now realised that a popular uprising in the form of mass civil disobedience is capable of matching, even defeating, the most powerful of military forces. While it is the PLO, under the leadership of Yassir Arafat, who have reaped the most diplomatic gains from the Intifadeh, it is the younger generation of local Palestinians who have taken the lead in the violent opposition. Approximately 50 per cent of the West Bank and Gaza Palestinians are under the age of 14, and over 70 per cent below 25. This is to say that they were born after (or shortly before) the events of 1967. Not only have they have never experienced anything other than occupation, a large percentage of them are highly educated and frustrated by both their political and economic subordinacy. These groups provide the nucleus for the spread of a more national political

Palestinian gunmen killed as intifada takes up arms

From Richard Owen, Jerusalem

The nightmare whic has haunted Israel's arm manders — that the ians would take up well as stones in became bloody r terday in a savage g West Bank village

The gunfire le soldier and thre gunmen dead. Strip, the Israel unrest moved with the arres cluding the t ers of the M talist move

Mr Yit Israeli Pr flies to L talks on proposa combin ... lec

some Palestinians will step up their battle for independence ... ing to weapons as and petrol

stumbled on Arab gunmen suspected of shooting Palestinian "collaborators", 40 of whom have been murdered since the uprising began.

The patrol came te car ca masked d army ve oldiers firin he car sudde he Arabs fir back window out to lob gre fire with an M Uzi machinegu

One Israeli geant, was killed nade, and the p mander, who wa lead vehicle, wa wounded by gunfi Palestinians were s the ensuing battle.

The gun battle

Mitzna said the dead Arabs came from Fatah, the mainstream faction of the Palestine Liberation Organiza: rectly

Have a carefree ride in areas: moving fortress for hire

By LARRY DERFNER
For The Jerusalem Post

TEL AVIV – And now for the latest in safe motoring through the occupied territories: the armoured truck.

For $50 an hour (or a cut-rate $35 an hour for six hours and up), lawyers, accountants, gold merchants and others who have business in the West Bank and Gaza can ride there inside the 7-cm.-thick steel-plated walls of "Chitov Security's" moured truck for hire.

Displayed at a news c here this week, the 4½-t 1978 Dodge was used for 10 the Bank of Israel to tran: billions of dollars in foreign the U.S. government deli Ben-Gurion airport. Afte 100,000 km, the truck was Chitov Security when th moved up to a 1988 Merce moured vehicle, said Shlomi man, the company's g manager.

'Collaborator' killed in village near Jenin

Vigilantes shoot up Halhoul

By JOEL GREENBERG
Jerusalem Post Reporter

A Palestinian man accused of cooperating with the Israeli security services was found dead at Ya'abad, Jenin yesterday. Palestinians Mustafa Hirzallah, 57, t of his house by ed to ques-

6 settlers held, more arrests likely in killing

By JOEL GREENBERG

Police were last night holding six settlers from Yitzhar south of Nablus on suspicion of involvement in Monday's raid on the rith, in which a was killed, and s wounded.

are apparently omb of Joseph s.

expected, as po er participants in working from a st of them yeshibok part in what "hike" through ettlers are being military govern , and their guns ted for ballistic

dents who were ay on Israel Ra-

the radio studios, and later appeared at a press conference. They told reporters that their group had opened fire in self defence, to drive back villagers who attacked them from rooftops with rocks, as soon as they entered the village.

An investigative team has been set up by the Samaria District police and is working in coordination with investigators from the Northern District.

It emerged yesterday that the two villagers wounded in the incident were not related to the girl killed and the house set on fire did not belong to her family, as originally reported.

Settler leaders last night condemned the arrests as "haphazard" and said they would continue to use their weapons in life-threatening situations.

In a related development, senior police officers complained yesterday

and in other recent incidents of settler retaliation, had noted the licence numbers of vehicles involved but made no effort to arrest the rioters, police officers said. This has made it impossible to pursue an investigation of several of the incidents, according to the police.

Michael Rotem adds:
Rabbi Yitzhak Ginsburg said yesterday in a telephone interview:
"I feel much better now, but this is not the point. I feel a mental pain because of the fact the Jews cannot walk safely in our father's land.

"We were going to pray on a holy grave when we were viciously attacked. I always taught my students that all of *Eretz Yisrael* is ours and ours only."

Asked whether he was sorry for the fatal shooting of the Arab girl, he evaded a direct answer by replying: "I regret the fact that Jews must

Over the 500 mark

The total number of Palestinians killed in the uprising topped 500 this week, according to unofficial casualty tolls. Statistics kept by Unrwa and foreign news agencies show at least 502 Palestinians killed. IDF statistics put the total at 475. Over 40 of those killed were slain by fellow Arabs who accused them of cooperating with Israel. Twenty Jews have been killed during the intifada, according to an unofficial toll. The IDF says 14 Jews were slain: eight civilians and six soldiers.

Figure 7.1 Collage of newspaper articles reporting the violent consequences of the Intifadeh
Source: *Jerusalem Post.*

consciousness amongst the local residents, arguing for more radical solutions – and hence active opposition – to the continued occupation.

Effects of the Intifadeh: the re-organisation of space

In practical terms, the Intifadeh has had a number of other effects on the Israel-Palestinian economy. In some cases, and for short periods of time, the local Palestinians have implemented a policy of economic disengagement. There are days on which the Palestinians may decide to withdraw their labour from the Israeli cities, while in the long term some Palestinians have ceased to commute into Israel altogether. Since the source of cheap labour is now an uncertain commodity, many Israeli employers have resorted to importing alternative labour from elsewhere on short-term contracts – most notably from Portugal and Poland. Tourism, a major component of the Israeli economy, has been severely damaged as many groups have cancelled their planned visits to the region owing to the violence. Since 1987, Christmas Eve in Bethlehem – the site of one of the major international tourist events in the calendar – has been a low-key affair, with relatively few visitors. This turndown in tourism has affected both the Jewish and Arab economies, especially in Jerusalem.

A second consequence of the Intifadeh is that the West Bank roads are no longer safe for Israeli travellers. Any Israeli car – identified by its yellow licence plates as contrasted to the blue plates of West Bank and Gaza Palestinians – is the target for stones or even a Molotov cocktail. While the average Israeli citizen - who may previously have driven through the West Bank in order to visit friends, go on an outing, shop in the Arab towns or simply as a short cut – can, and does, choose to travel on alternative routes within pre-1967 Israel, the Israeli settlers of the region have no such option. Having chosen to live within the West Bank and Gaza, they are obliged to travel on these roads in order to reach their homes and workplaces. The West Bank settlers have been on the receiving end of most of the stone-throwing incidents and they have become more radical, lobbying for the establishment of local civilian militias to patrol the roads and ensure the safety of their co-residents.

It is, as yet, unclear to what extent the Intifadeh

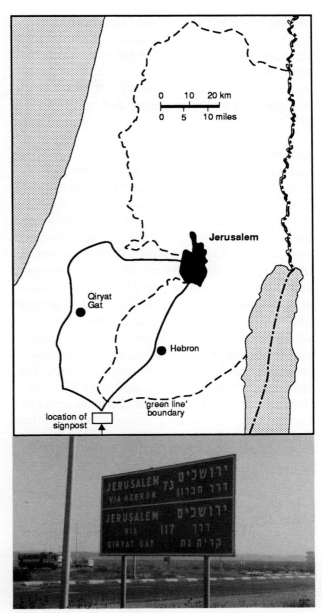

Plate 1 (with map) depicts the growing geography of fear which has grown up with the Intifadeh. A traveller on his way from the south of the country can choose between alternative routes. The shorter route – via the town of Hebron – takes him through the West Bank, while the longer route (over one and a half times as far) enables him to avoid the danger of being the target of a stone attack. Most travellers opt for the longer route. Thus the 'green line' boundary continues to play an important part in the route decisions taken by the individual traveller.

has caused a slowing down in the Jewish colonisation process. Initial data would seem to indicate that Israeli settlers have continued to move to the region despite the Intifadeh. But it must be remembered that the migration process usually involves the purchase of a land plot and the construction of a house, a process which often takes a few years. Thus the majority of those

48

moving to the West Bank and Gaza during the period 1987–89 had committed themselves prior to the onset of the uprising. The extent to which additional settlers have decided to settle in the region, in spite of the heightened tensions and increased fears, may be gauged during the early 1990s.

A third consequence, affecting the Arab sector, has been the significant loss of economic revenue. Since the Palestinian urban centres operate under a different set of restraints from the highly protected and socialised centres of economic activity within Israel, the former have become the focus for much economic interchange between the two sectors. Many comparable goods and services are cheaper within the Palestinian sector. Moreover, all places of commerce within Israel are closed on Saturdays (the Jewish Sabbath) while they remain open within the Arab centres. Some towns, particularly East Jerusalem, Bethlehem and Qalqiliyah, had become major foci for Israeli shoppers during the weekends, resulting in large profits for the local shopkeepers and restaurateurs. Since the onset of the Intifadeh, Israelis have ceased to travel to these areas for fear of their own safety, resulting in a major downturn in the economic activity of the local Palestinians.

Overall, the Intifadeh has served to bring the old 'green line' boundary – separating the West Bank from Israel between 1948 and 1967– back into focus, despite the fact that there is no physical sign of the boundary in the landscape, nor is it included in Israeli atlases and maps. Less interaction takes place between the two territories and their respective inhabitants, and the West Bank is increasingly perceived as a separate - albeit contiguous - territory. In the Gaza Strip, all local residents desiring to enter Israel have been issued with transit cards. These cards are scrutinised at the three checkpoints on the roads linking the Gaza Strip to Israel. Thus the Gaza Strip has reverted to a separate territorial entity, with clearly defined border crossings, access being limited to those holding valid transit permits. On certain days, such as public holidays in Israel, the West Bank and Gaza are declared 'closed areas' and the Palestinian inhabitants are prevented from travelling into Israel. It is, paradoxically, the hard-liners within Israel – those arguing for the continued retention and even declaration of sovereignty of the West Bank – whose policies of issuing transit cards to the Palestinians and closing the areas on certain occasions have brought the old

Figure 7.2 **Cartoon map images of the Intifadeh boundaries**
a) 'Borders 87' depicts the 'green line' boundary by means of Molotov cocktail incendiaries. The flaming bottle is at the town of Qalqiliyah where violent incidents had recently taken place.
b) 'The New Palestine' depicts the extension of the 'green line' boundary into Israel, to include the Arab-populated areas of the Galilee region. The boundary, in the shape of a serpent, is perceived as the dangerous importation of the Intifadeh into Israel proper.
Source: Ya'akov Shilo of the *Ma'ariv* (daily newspaper).

boundary back into clearer focus, thus emphasising the territorial distinctiveness of two separate territories.

A more serious consequence as far as Israelis are concerned is the effect that the Intifadeh has had on Israeli Arabs. On paper, Israeli Arabs share equal rights with Israeli Jews in all spheres of life. However, for the first decade following the establishment of the state, they were subject to rule by military government. Even when these restrictions were limited, they did not always enjoy the same benefits as the rest of the Israeli population. Many social welfare benefits in Israel are provided only to families in which the head of the household has served in the Israeli army (incumbent upon all Israelis over the age of eighteen). Israeli Arabs do not serve in the Israeli army, and hence are not entitled to many benefits. Similarly, the municipal status and budgets of Arab settlements often fall far behind the equivalent rates received by Jewish settlements. While Arabs comprise approximately 17 per cent of the Israeli population (within the pre-1967 boundaries), no Cabinet Minister (in a Cabinet of over twenty members) is an Arab. Yet there is a Minister responsible for 'Arab Affairs'.

Israeli Arabs thus feel discriminated against. They have begun increasingly to identify with the West Bank Palestinians during the past twenty years, as a result of free movement and interaction (including marriage) across the old 'green line' boundary. The younger generation of Israeli Arabs have also radicalised their stance and this has been reflected in recent voting patterns, fundamentalist Arab parties receiving a larger part of the vote. Within Israel, incidents of stone throwing at Israeli (Jewish) vehicles and other reported anti-government activities – albeit limited in number – have run parallel to the West Bank uprising. At the same time, more and more Israeli Arabs identify themselves as Palestinians, which was unheard of in the past. It is clear that the diffusive power of the Intifadeh has had no less a significant effect on Jewish-Arab relations within Israel itself.

It has been the Intifadeh and Israel's response to it which has, more than anything else, aided the Palestinian cause throughout the world. The perceived transformation of the PLO from a terrorist organisation to one representing a national struggle for independence, the declaration of the independent Palestinian state at the Algiers Summit of Arab leaders in November 1988 and the decision of the United States to hold informal meetings with representatives of the PLO have been spurred on by the popular uprising. For their part, Israeli leaders – following the setting up of a new national unity government in December 1988 – have been prepared to discuss the holding of free elections for West Bank Palestinians and even the withdrawal of military forces from certain built-up areas. While none of these proposals meets the demands for an independent Palestinian state – and to a certain extent they may be perceived as simply closing the stable door after the horse has bolted –

Plates 2 and 3. The Dahaishe Refugee Camp to the south of Bethlehem. These pictures show the changing roadside landscape of Intifadeh territory. Many of the refugee camps have been boarded up with sheets of aluminium in an attempt to prevent stones being thrown at passing vehicles. In Plate 2, the poor quality and high density of the refugee camp housing may be clearly seen, while in Plate 3 an Israeli flag on top of a roadside house is evidence of an army outpost – set up in an attempt to prevent further violent incidents.

there can be no doubt that their discussion now has been brought about by the understanding that the Intifadeh will not go away, nor can it be stamped out.

50

Postscripts

– On the morning of Sunday 20 May 1990, seven Palestinian workers were killed by a gunman on the rampage in the Israeli town of Rishon Letziyon. Within a few hours, the Intifadeh – having quietened down considerably during the previous few months – had returned in full force. Demonstrations, stoning of Israeli cars and army units, and violent police and military retaliation, resulted in a growing toll of dead and injured throughout the West Bank and Gaza Strip. Violent demonstrations and clashes also took place in Arab villages and towns within Israel, most notably in the Arab town of Nazareth in the Galilee region. The explosion of ethnic violence has once again demonstrated the underlying tensions felt by both Israelis and Palestinians, living on both sides of the 'green line'.

– In August 1990, the Palestinian leadership declared its support for Iraqi leader, Saddam Hussein, following his country's invasion of Kuwait. This step led to the suspension of the USA-PLO dialogue and a weakening of the Palestinian standing within the international community.

– On a bright October morning in 1990, Palestinian demonstrators threw rocks and stones at Jewish worshippers at the Western Wall. Israeli police opened fire, killing 21 of the demonstrators. The United Nations Security Council passed a unanimous resolution condemning the severe Israeli action. And so the violence continues . . .

– According to the human rights group, B'tselem, some 1,058 Palestinians, 50 Israelis and four Jewish tourists had died by the third anniversary of the Intifadeh in December 1990. Most of the Palestinians were killed by Israeli security forces. (*Jerusalem Post*, 7 December 1990)

Summary

• The Intifadeh (Palestinian uprising) commenced in December 1987 and has continued until the present date.

• Acts of violence (especially stone throwing) against Israelis have resulted in a strong-armed response on the part of the Israeli army. Despite their reputation as a strong and efficient fighting force, the Israeli army has been unsuccessful in its attempts to suppress this popular uprising.

• The existence of the Intifadeh has, for the first time since 1967, changed the nature of the relations between Israelis and Palestinians. The Palestinians often choose to withdraw their labour from the Israeli markets, while many Israelis will no longer travel through, or visit, the West Bank and Gaza for fear of their personal safety.

• Especially hard hit has been the international tourist trade to the Jewish, Christian and Muslim holy sites, particularly in Jerusalem and Bethlehem.

8   Political solutions

SINCE ISRAEL'S CONQUEST of the West Bank in 1967, various solutions have been proposed in an attempt to solve the conflict. These have ranged from the extremist Israeli positions (such as expelling all Arab residents of the region) to extremist Arab positions (a return to the pre-1948 geopolitics and the destruction of the Jewish state). Between the two extremes are a number of proposals, each of which requires compromise on the part of both sides. In this chapter, the territorial and demographic implications of seven solutions are discussed and compared.

Israeli annexation of the West Bank

Proposed by the Israeli right-wing, such a solution would necessitate the passing of a law in the Israeli Knesset – similar to that carried out for East Jerusalem in 1967 and for the Golan Heights in 1981 – formally annexing the West Bank. Israel would assume sovereignty over the West Bank thus providing the internal justification for the extension of Israeli civilian law to the region and its inhabitants. Despite the unilateral claim to such sovereignty, annexation would indicate Israel's ultimate intent of retaining the occupied territories. The border would remain, as at present, along the River Jordan in the east, separating Israel from the state of Jordan. In this way, Israel would use the West Bank as a buffer region between the armed forces of Jordan to the east and the major Jewish metropolitan centres along the coastal plain to the west.

While annexation provides a territorial solution as far as Israeli interests are concerned, it does not come to grips with the demographic problem. The extension of civilian law and Israeli sovereignty to the occupied territories would (assuming Israel's intent to retain a democratic state) necessitate the granting of full civilian rights to the Palestinian residents of the region. Allowing for the differential growth rates between Jewish and Arab populations, the latter (including Israeli Arabs) could become a majority during the next century, thus negating the *raison d'etre* of a Jewish state. In the survey carried out by the Jaffee Center for Strategic Studies (see Fig 2.3), only 18 per cent of the respondents were prepared to grant full and equal rights to the Palestinian inhabitants of the West Bank given annexation. Fully 49 per cent of the respondents argued that, even under annexation, the rights of the Palestinians should remain as they are at present, while a further 11 per cent wanted to decrease their rights (Arian *et al*, 1988, p.93). The extension of sovereignty to the territories and the refusal to grant full civilian and voting rights to the Palestinian population would be contrary to the ground rules of a democracy and would result in the creation of first- and second-class citizens.

One solution to this demographic contradiction is that put forward by the extremist Kach party under its former leader Meir Kahane, namely the expulsion of the local Palestinian population. The implementation of such a solution would leave the region *Arabfrei* and would thus 'solve' the demographic problem outlined above. This solution resolves the territorial question by dealing only with the human dimension. While the Kach party was not allowed to run for the Knesset in the 1988 elections owing to its racist manifesto, the basic concept of expulsion was adopted under another name, 'transfer', by the newly-formed Moledet party which subsequently gained two parliamentary seats.

An alternative to *de jure* annexation by Israel is the maintenance of the status quo – maintaining the process of *de facto* annexation. The setting up of Israeli settlements, the construction of spatial and economic infrastructure, the establishment of municipal regional councils and the gradual integration of the two economies, are all part of a process of creeping annexation. In view of the fact that formal annexation would create even more international criticism of Israel, as well as providing Israel with the formal obligation relating to the demographic problem, maintaining the existing situation is favoured by many settlers. Territorial presence, and hence control, is becoming more widespread over time, without obliging the Israeli government to grant equal rights to the Palestinian population as they do not reside in the areas claimed by Israeli sovereignty.

If we return to the survey of West Bank settlers carried out by Portugali and Newman in 1985, when presented with six possible political solutions to the future of the West Bank, some 42 per cent opted for formal annexation, while a further 33 per cent preferred maintaining the existing situation. While this is an unrepresentative sample of the Israeli population as a whole – it is to be expected that West Bank settlers will opt only for the right-of-centre solutions – by no means all of the respondents automatically opted for *de jure* annexation.

Allon Plan

This proposal, named after its author, former Deputy Premier Yigal Allon, has been the favoured policy of the Israel Labour party since 1967. If implemented fully, this solution would enable Israel to retain control over those parts of the territory perceived as being of strategic importance while, at the same time, dispensing with the moral obligations of administering the local Palestinian population. Allon proposed the creation of a double north-south line of Israeli settlements along Israel's eastern boundary with Jordan, in order to maintain physical control and provide 'defensible borders' for the country (Allon, 1976). The interior of the West Bank – the mountain ridge – in which the vast majority of the local Palestinian population resided, would not be colonised, and would become instead an autonomous Arab region linked to Jordan by means of an east-west territorial corridor. The autonomous region would thus form a territorial exclave, surrounded by an Israeli territorial presence. This proposal formed the basis of Labour government policy between 1967 and 1977, when a network of agricultural settlements was established along the Jordan Valley but not in other parts of the West Bank (see Fig 4.2).

The ability to implement the Allon Plan would depend on Jordan's willingness to retake control of the West Bank and its Palestinian citizens. But this possibility has become increasingly remote following the Palestinian declaration of an independent state in the region and King Hussein's announcement of Jordan's withdrawal from any active role in the West Bank. Nevertheless, a modified Allon Plan has continued to feature strongly in Labour party policy, as witnessed by the Labour party election manifesto in 1988. However, while the plan could possibly have been implemented prior to 1977 and the subsequent establishment of Israeli settlements throughout the region, it would now require the removal, or abandonment, of such villages and is therefore likely to be met with vehement opposition on the part of the settlers and their supporters.

Autonomy

The term 'autonomy' was first proposed in conjunction with the Allon Plan but it has since become associated with other proposals, especially those linked to the Camp David Accords between Israel and Egypt. This latter treaty included a clause promising the implementation of autonomy for the West Bank within five years of signing the Accords.

However, unlike the Allon Plan, in which the autonomous exclave would comprise both territory and people, the interpretation of the Camp David autonomy is unclear. Within Israel, there are two different interpretations. The right-wing camp hold that autonomy is limited to the human dimension – namely the Palestinians – while the territory would remain under Israeli control. In this way, Jewish settlers could remain in the region and the colonisation process could continue. In other words, there would be a dual system of citizenship for the residents of the region, Israeli (for Jews) and Jordanian (for Palestinians), while the territory would be retained by Israel. Issues such as municipal budgets, public services, education and so on would be in the hands of Jordan, while defence, security and probable control of water resources would remain with Israel. The alternative interpretation is that autonomy applies to both the territory and the people – similar to the Allon concept. In such a case, Jewish settlers would either have to leave their settlements and return to Israel, or accept non-Israeli citizenship. Israel would not retain direct territorial control within the autonomous region.

In a similar vein to the above two proposals, a study undertaken on behalf of the Center for Strategic Studies at Tel Aviv University by the political geographer, Saul Cohen (1986), has suggested a 'Map of Territorial Compromise'. Based upon the broader geopolitical context, rather than military considerations alone, Cohen argues that territorial adjustments should take the following six factors into consideration: 1) water control; 2) surveillance points, marshalling areas and corridors; 3) defensive depth; 4) growth space for population and economic activity; 5) absence of dense Arab population or barriers to such a population; 6) psychological or psycho-tactical elements that relate to the positioning of the boundary in the direct line-of-sight of substantial members of the Israeli populace. His proposals (Fig 8.1) cover 1,165 km² in Judea and Samaria

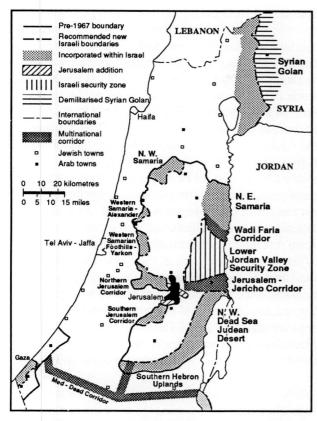

Figure 8.1   The map of territorial exchange
Source: Cohen (1986).

(20 per cent of the total area) plus a further 450 km² in the Lower Jordan Valley (security zone) and 200 km² taken for two multinational corridors. A third corridor (250 km²) would be taken from Israel.

Federation

Some scholars have suggested a federal solution to the Arab-Israel conflict, by which power would be shared by the antagonists. Federalism enables the separate and unhindered development of individual regions or provinces while maintaining a supra-state structure to which all belong and in which all are equally represented.

Two major models of federalism exist in the world today. The first of these is the United States model in which independent provinces decided to join forces for the mutual political and economic benefits of all, without handing over their individual sovereign powers to the central government. The second model, of which Switzerland is the classic example, is based on the separate autonomous development of regions, especially in cultural and educational spheres, as a

means by which the centrifugal forces of ethnic divisions can be overcome without dissolving the state altogether. A variety of federal solutions have been proposed as appropriate political solutions for ethnic conflicts in the Middle East region, including Cyprus, Lebanon and the Israel-Palestinian situation. In all three cases, the increasing territorial homogeneity and residential concentration of the conflictual ethnic groups provides the necessary geographical distribution amenable to a federal solution.

In a comprehensive study of the possibility of using a federal solution for the Arab-Israel conflict, political scientist Daniel Elazar (1988) has identified no fewer than eleven options. These range from a simple Israeli-Palestinian federation, an Israeli-Jordanian confederation and an Israeli-Jordanian condominium to bifederate arrangements, with or without Jordan. Federation, or even confederation, would enable regional self-rule for the dominant ethnic groups while, at the same time, enabling a territorial arrangement which would safeguard perceived military or strategic threats. In addition, such an arrangement would enable the three sovereign or autonomous units (Israel, Jordan and Palestine) to develop the regional economy to the mutual benefit of all sides. Arabs and Jews would be citizens of their own state or canton, while only matters of joint concern would fall in the sphere of the federal or confederal government. The proponents of federation argue that it would enable joint development projects (such as along the Aravah border between Israel and Jordan; joint water resource management; integration of West Bank labour and Israeli industrialisation) to be established. The major difficulty to be met in the formation of such an arrangement would be the need for an agreed security and defence policy.

Binational state

As we noted at the end of Chapter 2, few states in the world are mono-ethnic. Despite Israel being defined as a 'Jewish state', it possesses a significant non-Jewish minority – constituting some 18 per cent of the population within the pre-1967 boundaries and twice that number if the occupied territories are taken into account. The establishment of a binational Jewish-Arab state would acknowledge the reality of two peoples living within the same territory. In direct contrast to the solutions discussed thus far, all of which concentrate on some form of territorial and/or demographic separation between Israelis and Palestinians, a binational state would make territorial compartmentalisation meaningless. Any internal boundaries would be for administrative and planning purposes only and would not signify any form of ethnic or territorial separation. However, a binational state would also be the logical outcome of some form of federalism, in which the internal spatial divisions would reflect the dispersion of the different ethnic groups.

Under a binational solution, both Israelis and Palestinians would be equal citizens in a secular (not Jewish or Arab) state which would cover the entire territory as far as the River Jordan. While this solution was favoured by many groups prior to the establishment of the state in 1948, the radicalisation of the conflict during the past twenty years would appear to severely limit its attractiveness as a realistic solution for the present conflict. Moreover, the very essence of Zionism as a movement of Jewish nationalism is based on the premise of an independent Jewish state, with a Jewish majority. The rejection of this *raison d'etre* would be unacceptable to the vast majority of Israelis. In an era of growing religious fundamentalism – Muslim and Jewish alike – it is difficult to imagine the respective groups being sufficiently tolerant of the other concerning such diverse traits as language and religion. For an outsider, the binational solution may appear the most logical, while for a participant in the conflict it is probably the least acceptable.

Palestinian state in the West Bank

The formal declaration by the Palestinian National Council of an independent state in the West Bank in November 1988 heralded a new era in the Arab-Israel conflict. In territorial terms, the establishment of an independent state in the West Bank would mean the repartition of the region, similar to that existing prior to 1967. However, instead of falling under Jordanian jurisdiction, the Palestinian Arab inhabitants of the region would be full citizens in a separate and sovereign Palestinian state. The Jewish settlers would either have to leave the territory and return to live in Israel within the pre-1967 boundaries or become citizens of the new Palestinian state (an unlikely choice).

The formal PLO declaration refers to partition according to the United Nations 1947 partition resolution, rather than the post-1948 borders of Israel. Thus the proposed Palestinian state would be larger than that covered by the West Bank alone. Nevertheless, the PLO proposal should be seen as a bargaining point from which to negotiate as there is little support for such a stance outside the Arab world. At the same time, the 'green line' is by no means an optimal boundary. Various minor changes could be envisaged, involving both its physical straightening as well as territorial exchanges in micro-regions of Israeli Arab or Jewish settler concentrations. For example, the Arab residential concentrations on the Israeli side of the 'green line', such as the Little Triangle and the Umm el Fahm urban area, could conceivably be transferred to a Palestinian entity, while areas beyond the 'green line' containing Jewish settlements, such as the Etzion bloc south of Jerusalem or the southern Hebron settlements on the desert margins, could remain within Israel.

While the independent state solution is most logical in terms of sovereignty over the ethnic dominant territory, the economic viability of such a unit is questionable, particularly if the borders between the two entities were closed – thus preventing the free movement of people and goods. The West Bank is blessed with few natural resources, nor does it possess a self-sustaining industrial infrastructure. Open borders with Israel offer greater economic advantages (owing to the advanced industrial consumer economy in Israel and its link with European markets) than does a similar arrangement with Jordan. The current economic linkages are to the benefit of both sides – offering cheap labour to Israel and employment opportunities (albeit cheap menial labour) to the West Bank Palestinians – for at least as long as it takes for a vibrant local Palestinian economy to take shape.

The holding of free elections or a referendum amongst West Bank Palestinians concerning the future of the territory is certain to result in an overwhelming majority in favour of an independent state. Any national group desiring independence and political self-expression will not usually deny themselves that option because of a proven lack of economic viability. At the same time, the experience of many new independent nations has shown that the failure to provide a sound economic base, providing a reasonable standard of living and employment for most citizens, is often the recipe for political instability and internal revolution. Thus the question of economic linkages, industrial investment and access to global markets must also be addressed in discussing the nature of any independent state which may be set up in the future. But they are questions for the independent state to decide upon after having attained independence. They should not be used as a yardstick for determining whether or not to grant the independence in the first place.

Palestine Liberation Organisation (PLO) Charter

The extreme Arab solution is for the dismantling of the state of Israel, the expulsion of all Jewish immigrants and their descendants, and the creation of a single Palestinian Arab territorial entity with sovereignty over the whole of Palestine west of the River Jordan. This would include the return of Arab refugees from neighbouring Arab countries to their former homes, not only in the West Bank (post-1967 refugees) but throughout Israel (refugees from 1948 and their descendants; see Fig 2.8). In direct contrast to the Kach expulsion solution outlined above, the implementation of the PLO charter would make Palestine virtually *Judenfrei* and would negate the very existence of any Jewish entity in this region. When asked in the Jaffee Center survey (see Fig 2.3), what they believed the ultimate Arab aspirations to be, 36 per cent of the respondents answered that it was to 'conquer Israel', while a further 37 per cent felt that it was to 'conquer Israel and annihilate a large portion of the Jewish population in Israel' (Arian *et al*, 1988, p.100). Only 27 per cent believed that the ultimate aspiration was to regain some, or all, of the territories captured in the Six Day War.

It is the existence of the PLO charter (as well as the PLO terrorist/guerilla activities) which has formed the basis for Israel's opposition to holding talks with the organisation – even to the extent that Israeli law forbids meetings between Israeli citizens and known members of the PLO anywhere in the world. In October 1989, a well-known peace activist, Abie Natan, was jailed for six months for having met Yassir Arafat in an attempt to further the cause of peace in the region. Two months later Prime Minister Shamir attempted to sack Labour Party Minister Ezer Weizmann for having had unofficial contacts with PLO

representatives. Some Israelis assert that they would never be prepared to open direct negotiations with the PLO, but others hold that this situation would change were the charter to be formally annulled. While PLO sources argue that Yassir Arafat has, in fact, annulled the clauses calling for the destruction of Israel and the establishment of a single Palestinian entity, Israelis dispute this and argue that it is a propaganda exercise on the part of the PLO leader aimed at attracting world support. Nevertheless, events of recent years have led to an increasing number of Israelis and left-wing politicians openly stating their readiness to hold talks with the PLO.

In concluding this section, Table 8.1 provides a comparative analysis of the relative advantages and disadvantages of each of the solutions discussed above. But the objective analysis of pros and cons is not enough. It is also important to come to terms with the deeply ingrained opinions and perceptions held by the participants in the conflict. This was made clear in a further study carried out by scholars at the Jaffee Center for Strategic Studies (Alper *et al.*, 1989). This time, they examined the possibilities of achieving any one of six sets of political solutions. Their analysis was based on the identification of possible responses to each solution from the various participants in the conflict: Israeli Jews (right- and left-wing groups); Israeli Arabs; West Bank Palestinians; neighbouring countries; and so on. Their conclusion was that none of the solutions identified and commonly discussed held out any lasting hope of implementation, because there is always at least one group that is violently opposed to such an arrangement.

The first Jaffee Center survey discussed above (Fig 2.3) asked about the future of the territories – assuming peace negotiations with Jordan – and found that 49 per cent of the respondents answered that no territories should be returned, even for a peace agreement; only 16 per cent were prepared to return all the territories (allowing for minor border modifications and a special arrangement for Jerusalem) (Arian *et al*, 1988, p.92). While this sounds extremely pessimistic, it emphasizes the fact that any eventual breakthrough can be achieved only if both Israelis and Palestinians are prepared to make compromises. The alternative, the fulfilment of either of the ultimate solutions proposed by each side – would result in the total destruction and annihilation of the other.

Table 8.1: Summary of proposed political solutions

Proposal	*Implications for*	
	Israel	*Palestinians*
Expulsion of Palestinians	Retain extensive territorial control: demographic hegemony.	No independent state – major increase in numbers of refugees.
Annex occupied territory	Retain extensive territorial control: administer West Bank Palestinians. Offer equal rights – endanger Jewish majority.	No independent state – remain subordinate majority in West Bank.
Allon Plan	Territorial withdrawal from parts of the West Bank. Maintain control of Jordan Valley and East Jerusalem.	Autonomous rule in parts of West Bank – in conjunction with Jordan, linked by a territorial corridor.
Camp David autonomy	Retain extensive territorial control but without daily administration of inhabitants.	Autonomy for Palestinian residents but no control over home territory.
Federal solution	Relative autonomy and independence within separate territorial entities: possibilities include Israel and West Bank; Israel, West Bank and Jordan; Israel, Galilee, West Bank and Jordan.	
Repartition	Israeli withdrawal from West Bank. Galilee Arabs remain minority in Israel.	Independent Palestinian state in West Bank, within which there is a total Palestinian majority.
Binational state	Retain territorial wholeness of Israel and West Bank. Jewish majority will gradually dwindle.	Palestinian and Israeli Arab minority may eventually become a majority.
PLO covenant	Destruction of state of Israel. Jews become refugees.	Independent Palestinian state in whole of Palestine. Palestinian hegemony.

Summary

- Many political solutions to the Israel-West Bank problem have been proposed over the years. These range from extreme Jewish solutions (such as expelling the Palestinian inhabitants) to the extreme Palestinian solutions (such as the eradication of the state of Israel).

- Compromise solutions include such ideas as autonomy, repartition of Palestine/Israel into two states, and some form of federal arrangement between the two peoples.

- Each of the proposed solutions has at least one group who are opposed to its implementation.

9 Conclusions

ONE OF THE MAJOR PROBLEMS in attempting to present an analysis of an ongoing conflict is that events overtake the pace of publication. During the period in which this text was being prepared for publication (the first half of 1990), major political events took place within Israel and the West Bank.

Events since 1987 have substantially changed the conditions of the Arab-Israel conflict. The Intifadeh has been accompanied by a PLO declaration of an independent Palestinian state, while the PLO itself has become a legitimate participant in major international discussions, including those involving the USA. The new United States administration of President Bush, while declaring its commitment to Israel's right to exist in secure boundaries, is unlikely to share the same level of acceptance for all of Israel's actions as was the case under President Reagan. However, in the wake of the Iraqi invasion of Kuwait, international opinion has reverted in Israel's favour – until the next crisis!

For its part, Israel is no longer considered the 'victim' or the 'subordinate' partner in the conflict. The use of force in its unsuccesful attempt to quell the Intifadeh and its seeming inability to cross the psychological barrier of holding talks with the PLO has placed Israel in the category of 'lacking peaceful intentions' although for years it was the Palestinians and other Arab leaders who refused to sit at the same table as Israel. The broadly-based national unity government formed in November 1988 was headed by a Prime Minister and Foreign Minister, both of whom represent the hard-line camp which rejects all notions of a Palestinian state in the West Bank or of holding negotiations with the PLO.

At the same time, recent events have introduced a greater note of realism to all Israeli political circles, many of whom now realise for the first time the ultimate futility in attempting to control a growing, politically aware, Palestinian people. It must also be remembered that the Camp David Accords between Israel and Egypt were achieved by Prime Minister Begin, the first right-wing leader of Israel following thirty years of Labour party government. The idea that a gradual solution could initially be implemented by the present right-of-centre leadership should not, therefore, be discounted.

However, the highly tenuous nature of the Israeli political and electoral systems makes it extremely difficult for an Israeli government to adopt a well-defined peace policy. The electoral process consists of a nation-wide constituency in which the electorate vote for a singly party whose list of candidates has been drawn up by the party members themselves. The allocation of seats in the Israeli Knesset is directly proportional to the percentage of votes each party receives nation-wide. Thus a party polling 5 per cent of the votes will attain 5 per cent of the 120 seats in the Knesset. Under the existing system, a party only has to receive a minimal 1 per cent of the vote to obtain a seat in the Knesset. Thus many small parties contest the general elections and are able to obtain one or two seats in parliament. Such an outcome would not be problematic were either of the two major parties to obtain a clear majority of the seats (over 60), but this has never been the case in Israeli political history. Moreover, a virtual stalemate has emerged in recent years between the two major parties, making them totally dependent on a multitude of smaller satellite parties (often having no more than a single seat) if they are to succeed in putting together a ruling coalition government.

The elections of November 1988 centred around one issue only – the future of the West Bank and the Palestinians. As in the previous 1984 elections, the vote was fairly evenly split amongst parties of the right (favouring a hard-line policy) and of the left (favouring international peace negotiations, but not necessarily with the PLO). Since neither of the two parties was able to put together a convincing government with a clear majority in the Knesset, it was decided to have a 'national coalition' in which the Labour and Likud parties would share power, as indeed they had done for the previous four years. This coalition fell apart early in 1990, as a result of its inability to provide a positive answer to US Secretary of State, James Baker, in his endeavours to promote the peace process through a meeting of the Israeli, American and Egyptian foreign ministers in Cairo. This meeting was intended to provide the framework for the holding of free elections in the West Bank, enabling the Palestinians to choose a leadership which will represent them in talks with the Israeli government.

While the Labour party were eager to provide an immediate, and positive, response to the Baker Initiative, many of the hard-line Likud leaders insisted that such a response be conditional on receiving assurances from the Americans on the exclusion of East Jerusalem residents and known members of the PLO from the electoral process. Many Israeli leaders have gone on record as stating that they would continue to reject any notion of relinquishing Israeli rule over the West Bank; nor would they allow the participation of known PLO leaders or sympathisers. So far, the Palestinian leadership has rejected the proposal on the grounds that it does not go far enough. This, in turn, is interpreted by many Israelis as showing that the PLO is not really prepared to hold talks with Israel and that their recent public statements have been no more than attempts to bluff the international community. Both Israel and the PLO have demanded guarantees (which are unacceptable to the other side) from the United States as a pre-condition for further third party negotiations. In short, yet another stale-mate has been reached, this time resulting in the fall of the Israeli government in a no-confidence motion proposed by the Labour party themselves.

Following weeks of negotiations between each of the major parties with the smaller satellite parties, neither was able to put together a convincing government. Calls for the holding of early elections only held out the hope for more of the same, although if there were to be any shift in voting patterns, then recent trends would predict a minor swing in favour of the right (in a system where a swing of only one or two seats is of major significance). An analysis of the 'Jewish only' vote in recent Israeli elections shows a continued swing to the right-wing parties, including small extremist elements advocating 'voluntary transfer' of the country's Arab residents. This swing represents Israel's own radical reaction (especially amongst younger, first-time voters) to the increased radicalism it has encountered on the other side of the barricades, much of it in the form of young, educated, highly politically conscious, Palestinians.

For their part, Arab voting patterns within Israel display a continued swing away from Zionist parties to their own Arab lists. Despite the fact that Israeli Arabs represent some 18 per cent of Israel's population and that their leadership is democratically elected to the Knesset, many Israeli parties (especially of the right) refuse to undertake any form of coalition bargaining which includes the Arab parties. The commonly held perception of the 'Arabs' as a collective force, all of whom desire the ultimate destruction of the state of Israel, is often too strong for the Israeli Arabs to be considered as full political partners. This perception has become more pronounced in recent years as a result of some of the Arab parties publicly supporting Israeli dialogue with the PLO, as the only legitimate representatives of the Palestinian people.

Another factor which now has to be taken into account concerns the inflow of Jewish immigrants from Russia and eastern Europe. During the first half of 1990 alone, nearly 100,000 Jewish refugee immigrants arrived in Israel, while estimates for the subsequent two years spoke of hundreds of thousands of fellow travellers. This influx of population may have significant implications for the demographic question, discussed in Chapter 3. For their part, Arab leaders throughout the Middle East have attempted to exert political pressure through diplomatic channels to prevent any further immigration. Israel's major ally, the United States, has declared that it will provide financial aid and assistance for the resettling of the new immigrants only if Israel provides an assurance that they will not be settled in the occupied territories.

While the world focuses its attention on the question of the occupied territories, it is becoming increasingly clear that any political solution must attempt to take into account the whole gambit of relations between Israelis and Arabs throughout the region and not only in the West Bank. Politics and demography are intricately intertwined throughout and within geographical space. It is only within this unique spatial setting that the full implications of this bitter conflict between two national entities – each fully believing in its own rights to sovereignty over the same territory – can even begin to be understood. Were they to be implemented, elections in the West Bank could not be considered as constituting a full peace plan, although they do offer a short-term formula for breaking the present status quo – a status quo which is by no means static – and of advancing one small step in a positive direction. With the better part of a century of conflict behind them, it is obvious that any eventual solution requires a gradual, staggered, implementation. No short-term miracle will be able to provide the answers overnight.

Glossary of terms

ALLON PLAN – the name for the unofficial settlement policy pursued by the Labour governments of Israel between 1967 and 1977. Named after its proposer, Yigal Allon, the Plan limited its activity to the Jordan Valley, avoiding the densely populated upland regions.

BALFOUR DECLARATION – letter from British Foreign Secretary, Lord Balfour, to Baron Rothschild in 1918, assuring the latter of the British government's favourable disposition towards the eventual establishment of a Jewish homeland in Palestine.

BRITISH MANDATE – following the termination of World War I, parts of the area previously ruled by the Ottoman Empire were handed over – by international agreement – to Britain and France to administer for an undefined period of time. The area under British rule included Palestine. Due to the political tension and violence, Britain handed responsibility for this region back to the United Nations in 1947.

CAMP DAVID PEACE ACCORDS – peace agreement between Israel and Egypt, signed at the Camp David presidential retreat (in the USA) in 1979 between Israeli Prime Minister Menahem Begin, Egyptian President Anwar Sadat, and US President Jimmy Carter. In exchange for the peace agreement, Israel returned the whole of the Sinai Peninsula to Egyptian sovereignty.

GAZA STRIP – a small strip of land in the southern coastal plain, densely populated by Palestinian towns and refugee camps. Until 1967, this region was under Egyptian control, since when it has been under Israeli administration. It was not returned – nor requested – as part of the Camp David Peace Accords between Egypt and Israel.

GOLAN HEIGHTS – plateau overlooking northern Israel and the Huleh valley. Until 1967, part of Syria from which occasional attacks were made on Jewish settlements. Captured by Israel in the Six Day War, since when it has been settled by Israeli settlements. Considered a major strategic asset by Israel.

GREATER ISRAEL – territorial concept held by Gush Emunim and other like-minded territorial maximalists. The precise boundaries of this territory vary, but at their greatest extent stretch from the River Euphrates in the north-east, south to Wadi el-Arish in Sinai.

GREEN LINE – the name for the boundary separating Israel from the West Bank between 1948 and 1967.

GUSH EMUNIM – a religious-nationalist pressure group who believe in the divine right of the Jewish people to sovereignty over the whole of the 'Land of Israel' as defined in the Bible. Gush Emunim were the major proponents for establishing settlements throughout the West Bank during the 1970s and 1980s. Gush Emunim are vehemently opposed to any form of concession by Israel in the West Bank.

INTIFADEH – Palestinian popular uprising in the West Bank and Gaza Strip, commencing December 1987.

JORDAN VALLEY – easternmost margin of the West Bank forming the present boundary between Israeli- controlled territory and the state of Jordan. Part of the great Syrian-African rift valley.

JUDEA AND SAMARIA – the name used by Gush Emunim and Likud members to describe the West Bank. The name derives from the historical name for the Jewish kingdoms which existed in this region approximately 2-3,000 years ago.

LABOUR PARTY – the major left-of-centre party in Israeli politics. In power from the creation of the state in 1948 until 1977 and again as a coalition partner between 1984 to 1990. The Labour Party – at present headed by Shimon Peres – believes in territorial concessions in the West Bank and Gaza Strip in return for a peace agreement.

LIKUD PARTY – the major right-of-centre party in Israeli politics. Achieved power for the first time in 1977, since when it has remained in government. The Likud Party believe in retaining future control over the West Bank and are against any form of territorial concessions on the part of Israel. At the most, they are prepared to grant limited autonomy to the residents of this region. At the end of the 1980s, the party was headed by Prime Minister Yitzhak Shamir.

NOMAD LABOUR – term coined to describe the cheap labour who are not dependent on a specific place for their employment. They demonstrate great spatial flexibility and can thus move from one workplace to another with relative ease.

OPEN BRIDGE – policy put into effect by the Israeli military administration of the West Bank, enabling free flow of goods from the West Bank into Jordan.

OTTOMAN EMPIRE – Empire ruled from Turkey (the capital city was in Constantinople, now Istanbul) and including much of the Middle East; finally broken up following World War I.

PALESTINE – historically included the regions both west and east of the River Jordan. Following the creation of Transjordan in 1921, Palestine became the name for the area lying between the River Jordan and the Mediterranean Sea, administered by the British Mandate. With the establishment of the State of Israel, the name Palestine was used to denote the territory belonging to the Palestinians.

PALESTINIAN LIBERATION ORGANISATION (PLO) – umbrella movement for Palestinian organisations opposed to Israeli rule in any part of Palestine. Under the leadership of Yassir Arafat, the PLO undertook terrorist activities both in Israel and throughout the world. With the gradual increase in international recognition for the PLO during the 1980s, the organisation has also been involved in political and diplomatic activities.

SIX DAY WAR – the war which took place in June 1967 and lasted for six days. During this time, Israel conquered East Jerusalem, the West Bank, Golan Heights, Gaza Strip and the Sinai Peninsula.

SUBURBAN COLONISATION – settlements which are established for political reasons within a metropolitan hinterland, rather than in the periphery. Such settlements are able to attract relatively large numbers of settlers by exploiting the socio-economic processes of suburbanisation – that is, relatively cheap land within commuting distance of the major employment centres.

WEST BANK – name of the region west of the River Jordan, separated from Israel in 1948 by the 'green line' boundary. Between 1948 and 1967, the region was under Jordanian administration, since when it has been under Israeli control.

YISHUV KEHILLATI – dormitory and commuting settlement typical of the Israeli settlement models throughout the West Bank. The average settlement numbers between 100 and 200 family units.

Bibliography and sources

There are numerous books and articles on Israel and the West Bank, of varying quality and from different disciplinary perspectives. What follows is confined largely to geographical or geographically-related literature of recent origin which provides an up-to-date view and material of particular relevance to recent developments. Literature reflecting the different perspectives of Israeli and Palestinian scholars is mentioned. Also included are references to the sources from which information included in this *Update* has been derived.

In addition to the references listed below, the interested student should consult various issues of the *Journal of Palestine Studies*, *Studies in Zionism* and *Middle Eastern Studies* for differing analyses of the conflict and its history.

Suggested further reading

There are many introductory texts to political geography for the student unfamiliar with basic concepts such as 'the state', 'territory', 'ethnic groups', 'colonisation', etc. A recent comprehensive text is:

Glassner, M. and De Blij, H. (1989) *Systematic Political Geography* John Wiley, New York, fourth edition

This revised edition includes the most comprehensive bibliography on all topics of political geography.

For a wider regional perspective of the Arab-Israel conflict within the Middle East, it is worth consulting:

Beaumont, P., Blake, G.H. and Wagstaffe, J. (1989) *The Middle East: A geographical study* John Wiley, London, second edition (see especially Chapter 16, 433–459 'Israel and the occupied areas')

Drysdale, A. and Blake, G.H. (1987) *The Middle East and North Africa: A political geography* Oxford University Press, Oxford (see especially Chapter 9, 263–312 'The Arab–Israeli conflict')

For general material on Israel, Zionism and the Arab-Israel conflict, consult:

Gilbert, M. (1976) *The Arab-Israeli Conflict: Its history in maps* Weidenfeld and Nicholson, London, second edition

Khouri, F. (1976) *The Arab-Israel Dilemma* Syracuse University Press, Syracuse, New York, second edition

Orni, E. and Efrat, E. (1980) *The Geography of Israel* Israel Universities Press, Jerusalem, third edition

Sacher, H. M. (1976) *A history of Israel from the rise of Zionism to our time* Steimatsky, Jerusalem.

Accounts of the Palestinian refugee problem and the evolution of the Palestine Liberation Organisation (PLO) may be found in:

Cobban, H. (1984) *The Palestine Liberation Organization: people, power and politics* Cambridge University Press, New York

Morris, B. (1988) *The Birth of the Palestinian Refugee Problem, 1947–49.* Cambridge University Press, Cambridge

A descriptive analysis of changing socio-economic, political, demographic and settlement trends in the West Bank and Gaza Strip is to be found in:

Aruri, N. (ed 1984) *Occupation – Israel over Palestine* Zed Publishers, London

Benvenisti, M. (1984) *The West Bank Data Project: A survey of Israel's Policies* American Enterprise Institute for Public Policy Research, Washington.

Benvenisti, M. and Khayat, S. (1988) *The West Bank and Gaza Atlas* West Bank Data Base Project, Jerusalem Post Publications, Jerusalem

Elazar, D. (ed, 1982) *Judea, Samaria and Gaza: Views on the present and future.* American Enterprise Institute, Washington (Consists of nine essays on various aspects of the West Bank.)

Van Arkadie, B. (1977) *Benefits and Burdens: A report on the West Bank and Gaza economies since 1967* Carnegie Endowment for International Peace, Washington D.C.

Detailed source material
(includes all sources mentioned in text, plus additional research readings)

Abbu Ayash, A. (1981) Israeli planning policy in the occupied territories, *Journal of Palestine Studies,* 11 (1) 111–123

Abu Laghod, J. (1971) The demographic transformation of Palestine, in I. Abu Laghod (ed) *The Transformation of Palestine* Northwestern University Press, Evanston, Illinois, 139–163

Abu Laghod, J. (1982) Israeli settlement in occupied Arab lands: conquest to colony *Journal of Palestine Studies* 11 (1) 16–54

Allon, Y. (1976) The case for defensible borders, *Foreign Affairs* 55 (1) 38–53

Alper, J. *et al* (1989) *Judea, Samaria and Gaza: Israel's options for peace* The Jaffee Center for Strategic Studies, Tel Aviv University, Tel Aviv

Applebaum, L. and Newman, D. (1989) *Between Village and Suburb: New settlement forms in Israel* Settlement Study Centre, Rehovot, Bialik Publishers, Jerusalem (in Hebrew)

Arian, A., Talmud, I. and Hermann, T. (1988) *National Security and Public Opinion in Israel* Jaffee Center for Strategic Studies, No. 9. Tel Aviv University, Tel Aviv

Asadi, F. (1976) Some geographic elements in the Arab-Israeli conflict, *Journal of Palestine Studies*, 6, 79–91

Benvenisti, E. (1989) *Legal Dualism: The absorbtion of the Occupied Territories into Israel* The West Bank Data Base Project, Jeruslaem Post Publications, Jerusalem

Benvenisti, M. (1984) *The West Bank Data Base Project: A survey of Israel's policies* American Enterprise Institute, Studies in Foreign Policy, Washington

Benvenisti, M. (1989) *The Shepherds War: Collected essays (1981-1989)* West Bank Data Base Project, Jerusalem Post Publications, Jerusalem. (See especially Preface and Introduction, 1–34)

Bull, V. A. (1975) *The West Bank – Is it viable?* Lexington Books, Massachusetts

Cohen, S.B. (1977) *Jerusalem: Bridging the Four Walls. A Geopolitical Perspective* Westview Press, Boulder, Colorado

Cohen, S. B. (1986) *The Geopolitics of Israel's Border Question* Jaffee Center for Strategic Studies, Tel Aviv University, Tel Aviv

Coon, A.G. (1990) Development Plans in the West Bank *Geojournal* 21 (4), 363–373

Curtis, M. (1988/89) The Uprising's impact on the options for peace *Middle East Review* 21 (2) 3–11

Dahlan, A.S. (1989) Population, war and politics: A case study of the Gaza Strip, in Clarke, J.I. *et al.* (eds), *Population and Disaster* Basil Blackwell, Oxford

Dehter, A. (1987) *How Expensive are West Bank Settlements?* West Bank Data Base Project Jerusalem Post Publications, Jerusalem

Efrat, E. (1988) *Geography and Politics in Israel Since 1967* Frank Cass, London

Elazar, D. (ed, 1983) *From Autonomy to Shared Rule: Options for Judea, Samaria and Gaza* Jerusalem Center for Public Affairs, Israel

Falah, G. (1985) Recent Jewish colonisation in Hebron, in D. Newman (ed) *The Impact of Gush Emunim* Croom Helm, London, 245–261

Falah, G. (1989) The Israelisation of Palestine human geography *Progress in Human Geography* 13 (4) 535–550

Foucher, M. (1987) Israel/Palestine: which borders? A physical and human geography of the West Bank, in P. Girot and E. Koffman (eds) *International Geopolitical Analysis* Croom Helm, London, 158–195

Gerson, A. (1978) *Israel, the West Bank and International Law* Frank Cass, London

Grossman, D. (1986) *Jewish and Arab Settlements in the Tulkarm Sub-District* West Bank Data Base Project, Jerusalem Post Publications, Jerusalem

Harris, W. W. (1978) War and settlement change: the Golan Heights and the Jordan Rift, 1967–1977, *Transactions,* Institute of British Geographers 3 (3) 309–330

Harris, W. W. (1980) *Taking Root: Israeli settlements in the West Bank, the Golan and Gaza-Sinai* John Wiley, New York

Isaac, R.J. and Isaac, E. (1976) *Israel Divided* Johns Hopkins University Press, Baltimore

Kahan, D. (1987) *Agriculture and Water Resources in the West Bank and Gaza* West Bank Data Base Project, Jerusalem Post Publications, Jerusalem

Kipnis, B. (1987) Geopolitical ideologies and regional strategies in Israel *Tijdschrift voor Economische en Sociale Geografie* 78 (2), 125–138

Kliot, N. and Waterman, S. (1990) The political impact of writing the geography of Palestine/Israel *Progress in Human Geography* 14 (2), 237–260

Kollek, T. (1988/89) Sharing united Jerusalem *Foreign Affairs* 67 (2) 156–158

Levi, S. (1982) Local government in the administered territories in D. Elazar (ed) *Judea, Samaria and Gaza: Views on the Present and the Future.* American Enterprise Institute, Washington, 103–122

Matar, I. (1981) Israeli settlements in the West Bank and Gaza Strip *Journal of Palestine Studies* 11 (1) 93–110

Morris, B. (1987) *The Birth of the Palestinian Refugee Problem, 1947–49* Cambridge University Press, Cambridge

Nakhleh, E.A. (1979) *The West Bank and Gaza: Toward the making of a Palestinian state* American Enterprise Institute for Public Policy Research, Washington D.C.

Newman, D. (1982) *Jewish Settlement in the West Bank: The Role of Gush Emunim* Occasional Paper No. 16, Centre for Middle Eastern and Islamic Studies, University of Durham

Newman, D. (1984) Ideological and political influences on Israeli rurban colonization: the West Bank and Galilee mountains, *Canadian Geographer* 28 (2) 142–155

Newman, D. (1985a) The evolution of a political landscape: geographical and territorial implications of Jewish colonisation in the West Bank, *Middle Eastern Studies* 21 (2) 192–205

Newman, D. (ed, 1985b) *The Impact of Gush Emunim: Politics and Settlement in the West Bank.* Croom Helm, London

Newman, D. (1989) Civilian and military presence as strategies of territorial control: the Arab-Israel conflict *Political Geography Quarterly* 8 (3) 215–227

Newman, D. (1990) Overcoming the psychological barrier: the role of images in war and peace, in N. Kliot and S. Waterman (eds) *War, Peace and Geography* Pinter, London

Newman, D and Portugali, J. (1987) Israeli-Palestinian relations as reflected in the scientific literature *Progress in Human Geography* 11 (3) 315–332

Nijim, B. (1990) Water resources in the history of the Palestinian-Israel conflict *Geojournal* 21 (4) 317–323

Noble, A.G. and Efrat, E. (1990) Geography of the Intifada *Geographical Review* 80 (3) 288–307

Peretz, D. (1988) Intifadeh: the Palestinian uprising *Foreign Affairs* 66 (5) 964–980

Portugali, J. (1988) Nationalism, social theory and the Israeli/ Palestinian case, in R. J. Johnston, D. Knight and E. Koffman (eds) *Nationalism, Self-Determination and Political Geography* Croom Helm, London, 151–165

Portugali, J. (1989) Nomad labour: theory and practice in the Israeli-Palestinian case *Transactions,* Institute of British Geographers 14 (2) 207–220

Portugali, J. (1991) Jewish settlement in the occupied territories: Israel's settlement structure *Political Geography Quarterly* 10 (1)

Portugali, J. and Newman, D. (1987) *Spatial Interaction between the Israeli and Palestinian Populations of the West Bank and Gaza Strip* Ford Foundation Research Report, Tel Aviv

Reichmann, S. (1986) Policy reduces the world to essentials: a reflection on the Jewish settlement process in the West Bank since 1967, in D. Morley and A. Shachar (eds) *Planning in Turbulence*, Magness Press, Hebrew University of Jerusalem, 83–96

Romann, M. (1985) *Jewish Kiryat Arba Versus Arab Hebron* West Bank Data Base Project, Jerusalem Post Publications, Jerusalem

Romann, M. (1989) Territory and demography: the case of the Jewish-Arab national struggle *Middle Eastern Studies* 26 (3) 371–382

Romann, M. (1989) Divided perception in a united city: the case of Jerusalem, in Boal, F. and Livingstone, D.N. (eds) *The Behavioural Environment* Routledge, London and New York, 182–201

Rowley, G. (1983) Space, territory and competition: Israel and the West Bank, in Kliot, N. and Waterman, S. (eds) *Pluralism and Political Geography* St. Martin's Press, New York

Rowley, G. (1990a) The Jewish colonization of the Nablus region *Geojournal* 21 (4) 349–362

Rowley, G. (1990b) The West Bank: native water resource systems and competition *Political Geography Quarterly* 9 (1) 39–52

Sahliyeh, E. (1982) West Bank industrial and agricultural development: the basic problems *Journal of Palestine Studies* 11 (2) 55–69

Saleh, H.A.K. (1990) Jewish settlement and its economic impact on the West Bank, 1967–87 *Geojournal* 21 (4) 337–348

Sandler, S., and Frisch, H. (1983) *Israel, the Palestinians and the West Bank* Lexington Books, Massachusetts

Shilhav, Y. (1985) Interpretation and misinterpretation of Jewish territorialism in D. Newman (ed) *The Impact of Gush Emuunim.* Croom Helm, London

Soffer, A. (1984) The changing situation of majority and minority and its spatial expression - the case of the Arab minority in Israel, in N. Kliot and S. Waterman (eds) *Pluralism and Political Geography* Croom Helm, London, 80–99

Van Arkadie, B. (1977) The impact of the Israeli occupation on the economics of the West Bank and Gaza *Journal of Palestine Studies* 6 (2) 103–129